T0210603

Databases on Modern Hardware

How to Stop Underutilization
and Love Multicores

Synthesis Lectures on Data Management

Editor
H.V. Jagadish, *University of Michigan*

Founding Editor
M. Tamer Özsu, *University of Waterloo*

Synthesis Lectures on Data Management is edited by H.V. Jagadish of the University of Michigan.
The series publishes 80- to 150-page publications on topics pertaining to data management. Topics
include query languages, database system architectures, transaction management, data
warehousing, XML and databases, data stream systems, wide scale data distribution, multimedia
data management, data mining, and related subjects.

Databases on Modern Hardware: How to Stop Underutilization and Love Multicores
Anastasia Ailamaki, Erietta Liarou, Pınar Tözün, Danica Porobic, and Iraklis Psaroudakis
2017

Instant Recovery with Write-Ahead Logging: Page Repair, System Restart, Media
Restore, and System Failover, Second Edition
Goetz Graefe, Wey Guy, and Caetano Sauer
2016

Generating Plans from Proofs: The Interpolation-based Approach to Query
Reformulation
Michael Benedikt, Julien Leblay, Balder ten Cate, and Efthymia Tsamoura
2016

Veracity of Data: From Truth Discovery Computation Algorithms to Models of
Misinformation Dynamics
Laure Berti-Équille and Javier Borge-Holthoefer
2015

Datalog and Logic Databases
Sergio Greco and Cristina Molinaro
2015

Databases on Modern Hardware: How to Stop Underutilization and Love Multicores
Anastasia Ailamaki, Erietta Liarou, Pınar Tözün, Danica Porobic, and Iraklis Psaroudakis

ISBN: 978-3-031-00730-9   paperback
ISBN: 978-3-031-01858-9   ebook

DOI 10.1007/978-3-031-01858-9

A Publication in the Springer series
SYNTHESIS LECTURES ON DATA MANAGEMENT

Lecture #45
Series Editor: H.V. Jagadish, *University of Michigan*
Founding Editor: M. Tamer Özsu, *University of Waterloo*
Series ISSN
Print 2153-5418   Electronic 2153-5426

Databases on Modern Hardware

How to Stop Underutilization
and Love Multicores

Anastasia Ailamaki
École Polytechnique Fédérale de Lausanne EPFL

Erietta Liarou
École Polytechnique Fédérale de Lausanne EPFL

Pınar Tözün
IBM Almaden Research Center

Danica Porobic
Oracle

Iraklis Psaroudakis
Oracle

SYNTHESIS LECTURES ON DATA MANAGEMENT #45

ABSTRACT

Data management systems enable various influential applications from high-performance on-line services (e.g., social networks like Twitter and Facebook or financial markets) to big data analytics (e.g., scientific exploration, sensor networks, business intelligence). As a result, data management systems have been one of the main drivers for innovations in the database and computer architecture communities for several decades. Recent hardware trends require software to take advantage of the abundant parallelism existing in modern and future hardware. The traditional design of the data management systems, however, faces inherent scalability problems due to its tightly coupled components. In addition, it cannot exploit the full capability of the aggressive micro-architectural features of modern processors. As a result, today's most commonly used server types remain largely underutilized leading to a huge waste of hardware resources and energy.

In this book, we shed light on the challenges present while running DBMS on modern multicore hardware. We divide the material into two dimensions of scalability: implicit/vertical and explicit/horizontal.

The first part of the book focuses on the vertical dimension: it describes the instruction- and data-level parallelism opportunities in a core coming from the hardware and software side. In addition, it examines the sources of under-utilization in a modern processor and presents insights and hardware/software techniques to better exploit the microarchitectural resources of a processor by improving cache locality at the right level of the memory hierarchy.

The second part focuses on the horizontal dimension, i.e., scalability bottlenecks of database applications at the level of multicore and multisocket multicore architectures. It first presents a systematic way of eliminating such bottlenecks in online transaction processing workloads, which is based on minimizing unbounded communication, and shows several techniques that minimize bottlenecks in major components of database management systems. Then, it demonstrates the data and work sharing opportunities for analytical workloads, and reviews advanced scheduling mechanisms that are aware of nonuniform memory accesses and alleviate bandwidth saturation.

KEYWORDS

multicores, NUMA, scalability, multithreading, NUMA, cache locality, memory hierarchy

Contents

CHAPTER 1

Introduction

Ever-increasing data volumes and the complexity of queries posed over the data are requiring increased processing power from the database management systems (DBMS). While modern hardware keeps offering increased parallelism and capabilities, harnessing them has been a perpetual challenge for decades. In particular, hardware trends oblige software to overcome three major challenges against systems scalability:

1. exploiting the abundant thread-level parallelism provided by multicores;

2. achieving predictably efficient execution despite the non-uniformity in multisocket multicore systems; and

3. taking advantage of the aggressive microarchitectural features.

In this book, we shed light on these three challenges and survey recent proposals to alleviate them. We divide the material into two dimensions of scalability in a single multisocket multicore hardware: implicit/vertical and explicit/horizontal.

1.1   IMPLICIT/VERTICAL DIMENSION

Figure 1.1 illustrates the implicit/vertical dimension of multicore hardware. The scalability of this dimension refers to utilizing the resources of a single core more effectively.

In step with Moore's law [99], processor technology has gone through major advancements over the years. Prior to 2005, hardware vendors mainly innovated on implicit parallelism within a core boosting the performance of a single thread (Figure 1.1 left-hand side). They either kept clocking the processors at higher frequencies or designing aggressive microarchitectural features (e.g., long execution pipelines, super-scalar execution, out-of-order execution, branch prediction, vector processing, etc. [59]) that increase the complexity of a processor. However, taking advantage of such features is never straightforward for the complex data management applications [8, 54], mainly due to the low instruction level parallelism (ILP) they exhibit. These applications usually require fundamental algorithmic changes in order to really exploit both data- and instruction-level parallelism opportunities that exist on modern processors [78, 130, 134].

The algorithmic changes that take into account the microarchitectural features of a core are only one part of the solution. One also needs to account for the memory hierarchy on the machines being used (Figure 1.1 right-hand side). Recent studies analyzing the microarchitectural behavior of typical data management workloads on modern hardware emphasize that more than

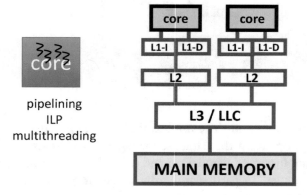

Figure 1.1: The implicit/vertical scalability dimension refers to optimizing the performance of DBMS by increasing the utilization of cores and caches.

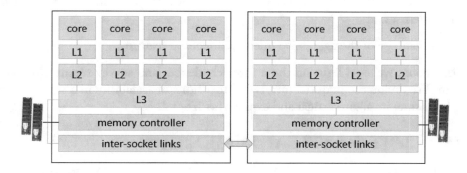

Figure 1.2: The explicit/horizontal scalability dimension refers to optimizing the performance of DBMS by better utilizing the increasing number of cores and sockets.

half of the execution time goes to memory stalls when running data-intensive workloads [42]. As a result, on processors that have the ability to execute four instructions per cycle (IPC), which is common for modern commodity hardware, data intensive workloads, especially transaction processing, achieve around one instruction per cycle [141, 152]. Such underutilization of microarchitectural features is a great waste of hardware resources.

Several proposals have been made to reduce memory stalls through improving instruction and data locality to increase cache hit rates. For data, these range from cache-conscious data structures and algorithms [30] to sophisticated data partitioning and thread scheduling [115]. For instructions, they range from compilation optimizations [131], and advanced prefetching [43], to computation spreading [13, 26, 150] and transaction batching for instructions [14, 55]. In addition, several recent proposals opt for hardware specialization for some of the database operations [65, 85, 166].

1.2   EXPLICIT/HORIZONTAL DIMENSION

Figure 1.2 illustrates the explicit/horizontal dimension of multicore hardware. The scalability of this dimension refers to utilizing the increasing number of cores and sockets in a single multi-socket multicore server hardware.

Since the beginning of this decade, power draw and heat dissipation prevent processor vendors from relying on rising clock frequencies or more aggressive microarchitectural techniques for higher performance. Instead, they add more processing cores or hardware contexts on a single processor to enable exponentially increasing opportunities for parallelism [107]. Exploiting this parallelism is crucial for utilizing the available architectural resources and enabling faster software. However, designing scalable systems that can take advantage of the underlying parallelism remains a challenge. In traditional high-performance transaction processing, the inherent communication leads to scalability bottlenecks on today's multicore and multisocket hardware. Even systems that scale very well on one generation of multicores might fail to scale-up on the next generation. On the other hand, in traditional online analytical processing, the database operators that were designed for unicore processors fail to exploit the abundant parallelism offered by modern hardware.

Servers with multiple processors and non-uniform memory access (NUMA) design present additional challenges for data management systems, many of which were designed with implicit assumptions that core-to-core communication latencies and core-to-memory access latencies are constant regardless of location. However, today for the first time we have *Islands*, i.e., groups of cores that communicate fast among themselves and slower with other groups. Currently, an Island is represented by a processor socket but soon, with dozens of cores on the same socket, we expect that Islands will form within a chip. Additionally, memory is accessed through memory controllers of individual processors. In this setting, memory access times vary greatly depending on several factors including latency to access remote memory and contention for the memory hierarchy such as the shared last level caches, the memory controllers, and the interconnect bandwidth.

Abundant parallelism and non-uniformity in communication present different challenges to transaction and analytical workloads. The main challenge for transaction processing is communication. In this part of the book, we initially teach a methodology for scaling up transaction processing systems on multicore hardware. More specifically, we identify three types of communication in a typical transaction processing system: *unbounded, fixed, and cooperative* [67]. We demonstrate that the key to achieving scalability on modern hardware, especially for transaction processing systems, but also for any system that has similar communication patterns, depends on avoiding the unbounded communication points or downgrading them into fixed or cooperative ones. We show how effective this methodology is in practice by surveying related proposals from recent work (e.g., [36, 76, 109, 146, 149, 158]).

Non-uniform communication latencies make it appealing to regard multisocket as a distributed system and deploy multiple nodes in a shared-nothing configuration [76, 146]. While this approach works great for perfectly partitionable workloads, it is very sensitive to distributed transactions and the workload skew. At the same time, hardware-oblivious shared-everything systems suffer from non-uniform latencies that amplify bottlenecks in the critical path [116]. In order to achieve scalability on multisockets one needs to make the system aware of the hardware topology and dynamically adapt to workload and hardware [115].

On the other hand, traditional online analytical processing workloads are formed of scan-heavy, complex, ad-hoc queries that do not suffer from the unbounded communication as in transaction processing. Analytical workloads are still concerned with the variability of latency, but also with avoiding saturating resources such as memory bandwidth. In many analytical workloads that exhibit similarity across the query mix, sharing techniques can be employed to avoid redundant work and re-use data in order to better utilize resources and decrease contention. We survey recent techniques that aim at exploiting work and data sharing opportunities among the concurrent queries (e.g., [22, 48, 56, 119]).

Furthermore, another important aspect of analytical workloads, in comparison to transaction processing, is the opportunity for intra-query parallelism. Typical database operators, such as joins, scans, etc., are mainly optimized for single-threaded execution. Therefore, they fail to exploit intra-query parallelism and cannot utilize several cores naïvely. We survey recent parallelized analytical algorithms on modern non-uniform, multisocket multicore architectures [9, 15, 94, 127].

Finally, in order to optimize performance on non-uniform platforms, the execution engine needs to tackle two main challenges for a mix of multiple queries: (a) employing a scheduling strategy for assigning multiple concurrent threads to cores in order to minimize remote memory accesses while avoiding contention on the memory hierarchy; and (b) dynamically deciding on the data placement in order to minimize the total memory access time of the workload. The two problems are not orthogonal, as data placement can affect scheduling decisions, while scheduling strategies need to take into account data placement. We review the requirements and recent techniques for highly concurrent NUMA-aware scheduling for analytics, which take into consideration data locality, parallelism, and resource allocation (e.g., [34, 35, 91, 122]).

1.3   STRUCTURE OF THE BOOK

In this book, we aim to examine the following questions.

- How can one adapt traditional execution models to fully exploit modern hardware?

- How can one maximize data and instruction locality at the right level of the memory hierarchy?

- How can one continue scaling-up despite many cores and non-uniform topologies?

We divide the material into two parts based on the two dimensions of scalabilty defined above.

Part I focuses on implicit/vertical dimension of scalability. It describes the resources offered by the modern processor cores and deep memory hierarchies, explains the reasons behind their underutilization, and offers ways to improve their utilization while also improving the overall performance of the systems running on top. In this first part, Chapter 2 first gives an overview of the instruction and data parallelism opportunities in a core, and presents key insights behind techniques that take advantage of such opportunities. Then, Chapter 3 discusses the properties of the typical memory hierarchy of a server processor today, and illustrates the strengths and weaknesses of the techniques that aim to better utilize microarchitectural resources of a core.

Part II focuses on explicit/horizontal dimension of scalability. It separately explores scalability challenges for transactional and analytical applications, and surveys recent proposals to overcome them. In this second part, Chapter 4 delves into the scalability challenges of transaction processing applications on multicores and surveys a plethora of proposals to address them. Then, Chapter 5 investigates the impact of bandwidth limitations in modern servers and presents a variety of approaches to avoid them.

Finally, Chapter 6 discusses some related hardware and software trends and provides an outlook of future directions. Chapter 7 concludes this book.

PART I

Implicit/Vertical Scalability

CHAPTER 2

Exploiting Resources of a Processor Core

In this chapter, we discuss parallelism opportunities in modern CPUs. We cover all the topics shown in Figure 2.1. First, we show that parallelization already exists inside a single-threaded CPU core. We give a brief overview of instruction pipelining, and we explain superscalar and SIMD processors. Then, we move a step further to CPUs with more than one hardware thread inside a single core, the implications of simultaneous multithreading/hyperthreading, and how to utilize this architecture. Finally, we describe how we can efficiently achieve horizontal parallelism in multicores.

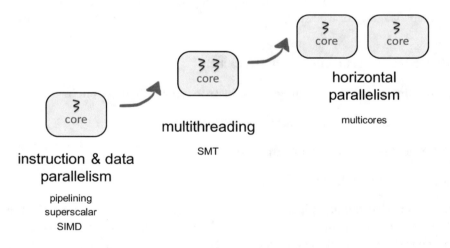

Figure 2.1: The different parallelism opportunities of modern CPUs.

2.1 INSTRUCTION AND DATA PARALLELISM

In the early times of processors, a CPU executed only one machine instruction at a time. Only when a CPU was completely finished with an instruction it would continue to the next instruction. This type of CPU, usually referred to as "subscalar," executes one instruction on one or two pieces of data at a time. In the example of Figure 2.2, the CPU needs ten cycles to complete two instructions.

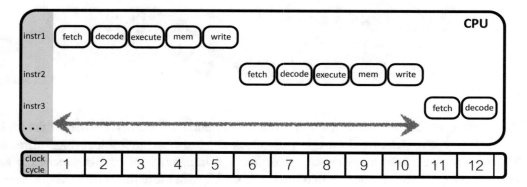

Figure 2.2: Subscalar CPUs execute one instruction at a time.

The execution of an instruction is not a monolithic action. It is decomposed into a sequence of discrete steps/stages. For example, the classic RISC pipeline consists of the following distinct phases:

- FETCH: fetch the instruction from the cache.

- DECODE: determine the meaning of the instruction and register fetch.

- EXECUTE: perform the real work of the instruction.

- MEMORY: access an operand in data memory.

- WRITE BACK: write the result into a register.

There are designs that include pipelines with more stages, e.g., 20 stages on Pentium 4. Each pipeline stage works on one instruction at a time. We can think of the stages as different workers that each one is doing something different in each functional unit of the CPU. For example, in subscalar CPUs, when the CPU is on the decode stage, only the relevant functional unit is busy and the other functional units of the other stages are idle. For this reason, most of the parts of a subscalar CPU are idle most of the time.

One of the simplest methods used to accomplish increased parallelism is with instruction pipelining (IPL). In this method, we shift the instructions forward, such that they can partially overlap. In this way, as shown in Figure 2.3, we can start the first step of an instruction before the previous instruction finishes executing. For example, in the fourth cycle of Figure 2.3 there are four instructions in the pipeline, each of which is on a different stage. With instruction pipelining, only six cycles are needed to execute two instructions, while the subscalar CPU needs

10 cycles for the same amount of work, as we show in Figure 2.2. Note, with IPL the instruction latency is not reduced; we still need to go through all the steps and spend the same number of cycles to complete an instruction. The major advantage of IPL is that the instruction throughput is increased, i.e., in the same time more instructions are completed. A CPU is called "fully pipelined" if it can fetch an instruction on every cycle.

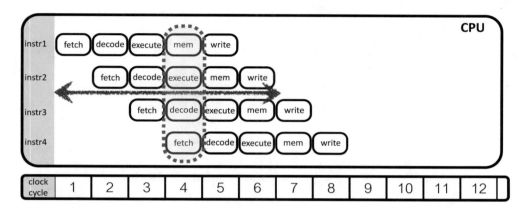

Figure 2.3: With instruction pipelining, multiple instructions can be partially overlapped.

Today, we have "superscalar" CPUs that can execute more than one instruction during a clock cycle by simultaneously issuing multiple instructions. Each instruction processes one data item, but there are multiple redundant functional units within each CPU, thus multiple instructions can process separate data items concurrently. Each functional unit is not a separate CPU core but an execution resource within a single CPU. Figure 2.4 shows an example of a superscalar CPU that can issue four instructions at the same time. In this way, instruction parallelism can be further increased.

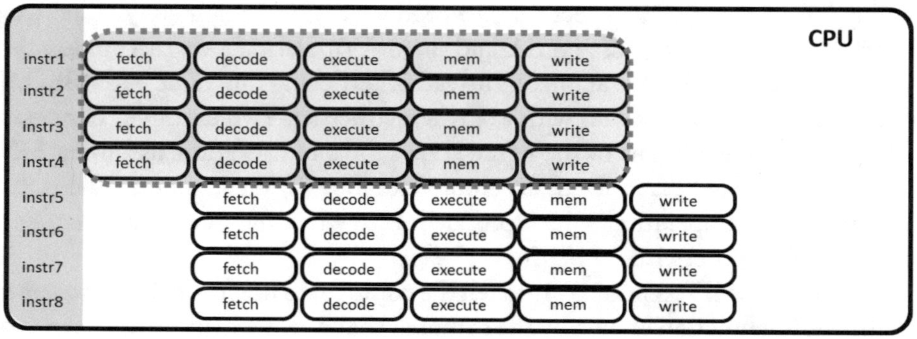

Figure 2.4: A superscalar CPU can issue more than one instruction at a time.

So far, we discussed how to increase CPU utilization by widening the instruction parallelism. Each instruction is operating on a single data item. Such traditional instructions are called single instruction single data (SISD). Parallelization, however, can be further increased on the data level. There are CPUs that can issue a single instruction over multiple data items, which are called single instruction multiple data (SIMD). In Figure 2.5 we show the input and output of both SISD and SIMD designs.

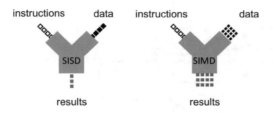

Figure 2.5: A single SIMD instruction can be issued over multiple data items.

SIMD instructions reduce compute-intensive loops by consuming more data per instruction. If we let K denote the degree of available parallelism, i.e., the number of words that fit in a SIMD register, we can achieve a performance speed-up of K. The advantage here is that there are fewer instructions, which means less overall fetching and decoding phases. SIMD is efficient in processing large arrays of numeric values, e.g., adding/subtracting the same value to a large number of data points. This is applicable to many multimedia applications, e.g., changing the brightness of an image, where we need to modify each pixel of the image in the same way.

In order to better understand the difference between SISD and SIMD instructions, assume that we need to feed the result of an operation "op" with an input from two vectors A and B, into a result vector R, as shown in Figure 2.6. With SISD, we first need to take the first value from A and B (i.e., A1 and B1, respectively) to produce the first result (R1). Then we proceed with the next pair of values, i.e., A2 and B2, and so on. With SIMD, we can process the data in blocks (a chunk of values is loaded at once). Instead of retrieving one value with SISD, a SIMD processor can retrieve multiple values with a single instruction. Two examples of operations are shown in Figure 2.7. The left part of the figure shows the sum operation; assuming SIMD registers of 128 bits, it means that we can accommodate four 32-bit numbers. The right part of the figure shows the min operation, which produces zero when the first input is larger than the second, or 32 bits of 1 otherwise.

The way to use SIMD technology is to tell the compiler to use intrinsics to generate SIMD code. An intrinsic is a function known by the compiler that directly maps to a sequence of one or more assembly language instructions. For example, consider the transformation of the following loop that sums an array:

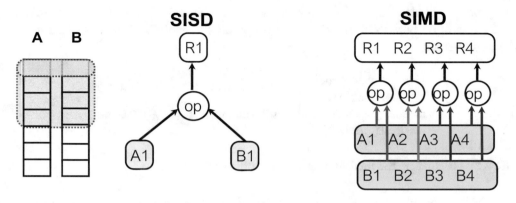

Figure 2.6: SISD vs. SIMD instructions for an operation that operates on the values of two vectors.

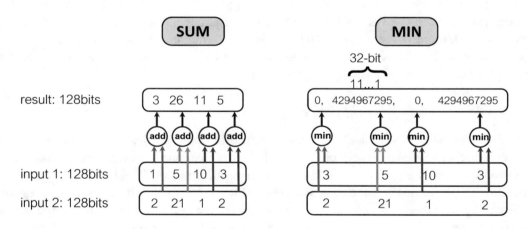

Figure 2.7: 128-bit SIMD instructions for adding pairs of values from two vectors, and for finding the minimum of pairs of values from two vectors.

```
for(i=0;i<N;i++)              for (i=0;i<N;i+=4)
  res+=a[i]         ⟶          res[i,i+1,i+2,i+3]=
                              SIMD_add(res[i,i+1,i+2,i+3], a[i,i+1,i+2,i+3])
```

The transformed loop (on the right) executes four times less instructions. A difference between the two loops, however, is that the transformed loop does not calculate a single result sum, but four partial ones, i.e., instead of calculating the single value res, we have the array res[N-4, N-3, N-2, N-1]. The way to continue with SIMD registers from this point is to use SIMD shuffle instructions [172], as shown in Figure 2.8. The 32-bit shuffle version interchanges the first group of 32 bits to the second group of 32 bits, and the third group of 32 bits to the fourth group of 32 bits. The 64-bit shuffle version interchanges the first group of 64 bits to the second group of 64 bits. With the shown instructions, the final 32-bit sum appears four times in the result vector.

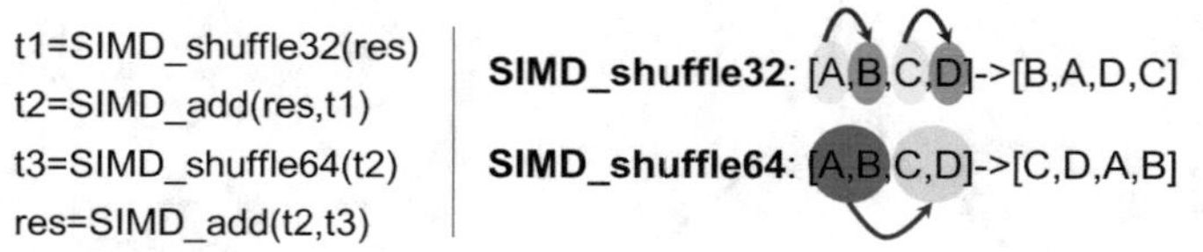

```
t1=SIMD_shuffle32(res)      SIMD_shuffle32: [A,B,C,D]->[B,A,D,C]
t2=SIMD_add(res,t1)
t3=SIMD_shuffle64(t2)       SIMD_shuffle64: [A,B,C,D]->[C,D,A,B]
res=SIMD_add(t2,t3)
```

Figure 2.8: Calculating the final sum result by shuffling partial results.

SIMD instructions are an excellent match for applications with a large amount of data parallelism, e.g., column stores. Many common operations are amenable SIMD style parallelism, including partitioning [114], sorting [137], filtering [113, 142], and joins [78]. More modern instructions sets, such as AVX2 and AVX-512, support gather and scatter instructions that fetch data from, and, respectively, save data to multiple non-contiguous memory locations. This kind of instruction makes it easier for row stores to exploit SIMD too, where the data we need to process may not be in a contiguous memory area [113].

2.2 MULTITHREADING

After discussing single-core, single-threaded parallelism opportunities, let us move a step forward and discuss how one can exploit CPUs with more than one hardware thread in the same core (middle level of Figure 2.1). In simultaneous multithreading (SMT), there are multiple hardware threads inside the same core, as shown in Figure 2.9. Each thread has its own registers (indicated by the green and blue dots in Figure 2.9, for the green and the blue colored thread, respectively) but they still share many of the execution resources, including the memory bus and the caches. In this way, it is like having two logical processors. Each thread is reading and executing instructions of its own instruction stream. SMT is a technique proposed to improve the overall efficiency of CPUs. If one thread stalls, another can continue. In this way, CPU resources can continue to be utilized. But this is not always an easy goal to achieve, we need to schedule properly multiple hardware threads. Next, we explore three different approaches of how we can take advantage of the SMT architecture [171].

One approach is to treat logical processors as physical, namely as having multiple real physical cores in the CPU, and treat the SMT system as a multiprocessor system. In Figure 2.10a, we show two tasks, A and B, that are assigned to the green and the blue thread, respectively. Think of tasks A and B as any data-intensive database operation, such as aggregations and joins, that can run independently, e.g., the same operator is being run in each thread, but each operator has its own input and output data. The advantage of this approach is that it requires minimal code changes; in case our application is already multithreaded this approach is coming almost

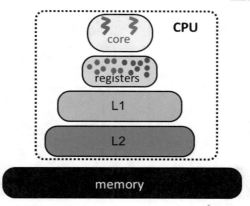

Figure 2.9: Multiple hardware threads inside the same CPU core.

for free. We can assign a software thread to a hardware thread. The disadvantage, however, is that in this way resource sharing, such as caches, is ignored. In Figure 2.10a, we show that both threads are competing for L1 and L2 caches. This fact can eventually lead to over-use and contention of shared resources; when threads compete with each other for a shared resource, overall performance may be decreased.

Another approach is to assign different parts of the same task to all hardware threads, implementing operations in a multithreaded fashion. In this case, as shown in Figure 2.10b, we split the work of task A in half, such as the green thread handles the first half of the task and the blue thread handles the other half. For example, task A could be an aggregation operation where the green thread processes the odd tuples and the blue thread processes the even tuples of the input. The advantage of this approach is that running one operation at a time on an SMT processor might be beneficial in terms of data and instruction cache performance. The disadvantage, however, is that we need to rewrite our operators in a multithreaded fashion. One tricky point of this approach is how the two threads will collaborate for completing the same goal (i.e., task A). Namely, how we can handle the partitioning and merging of the partial work. As mentioned before, one way to avoid conflicts on input is to divide the input and use a separate thread to process each part; for example, one thread handles the even tuples, and the other thread handles the odd tuples. Sharing the output is more challenging, as thread coordination is required. If the two threads were to write to a single output stream, they would frequently experience write-write contention on common cache lines. This contention is expensive and negates any potential benefit of multithreading. Instead, we can implement the two threads with separate output buffers, so that they can write to disjoint locations in memory. When both threads finish, the next operator needs to merge the partial results. In this way, we may lose the order of the input tuples, which can be significant for the performance of some operations, e.g., binary search.

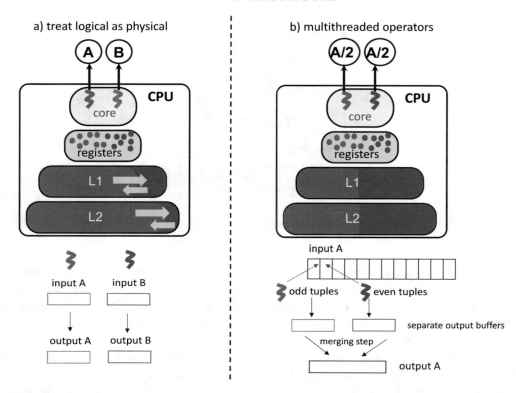

Figure 2.10: Two alternative ways of using SMT.

The third alternative approach of exploiting the SMT architecture employs two hardware threads that are collaborating to finish the work faster and with less cache misses. The collaboration happens not by dividing the work as seen before, but by assigning different roles to each thread. According to the approach, proposed in [171], the first thread, called the main worker thread is responsible to do the actual work, the main CPU computation. The second thread is called the helper thread and performs aggressive data preloading, namely it brings the data elements that the worker thread is going to need soon, as shown in Figure 2.11. In this way, the helper thread suffers more from the memory latency while the main thread is free of that and it is able to work on the real computation. To achieve this, we need a common point of reference for both threads, this is the "work-ahead" data structure, where the worker (green) thread adds what is the next memory address it is going to need. Once it submits the request, it continues with other work instead of waiting for that memory address right away. The helper thread goes through the "work-ahead set" and brings the addresses back.

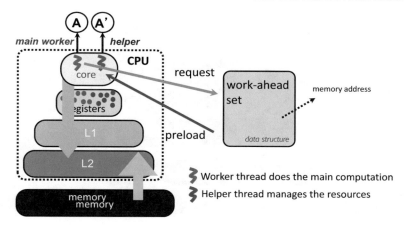

Figure 2.11: Third alternative way of using SMT.

To sum up, the performance of a SMT system is intrinsically higher than when we have a single core with a single thread. Of course, one needs to carefully schedule and assign the proper task to each thread. Nevertheless, since two logical threads share resources, they can never be better than having two physical threads as in the case of multicore CPUs that we see next.

2.3   HORIZONTAL PARALLELISM

In this section, we move one more step forward (last level of Figure 2.1) to discuss parallelism opportunities in multicore CPUs. In a multicore CPU, there are multiple physical cores, as shown in Figure 2.12. Each core has its own registers and private caches, and they all share the LLC. The fundamental question that needs to be answered here is how to keep the multicore CPU at 100% utilization. The improvement in performance gained by the use of a multicore processor depends heavily on the software algorithms used and their implementation. In the best case scenario, e.g., for "embarrassingly parallel" problems, we can have a speed-up factor that approaches the number of cores. In the remaining of the chapter, we discuss a few key cases of how multicore CPUs can be employed.

Assume the scenario that multiple similar queries start scanning a table at the same time. One approach to execute the queries, is by assigning each query to a core [127], i.e., core 0 is responsible for query Q1, core 1 is responsible for query Q2, etc., as shown in Figure 2.13. In this approach, Q1 may incur a cache miss to read each tuple from main memory, while Q2-Q4 take advantage of the data Q1 has read into the processor's shared LLC. Slower queries can catch up. Faster queries wait for the memory controller to respond. In this way, each core has to go through all the data blocks for executing just one query. So the cores go through the

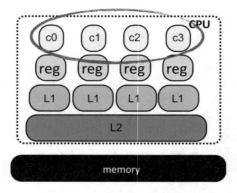

Figure 2.12: Multicore CPU have multiple cores that can work in parallel.

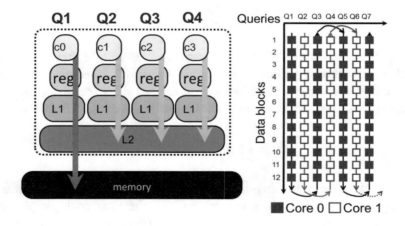

Figure 2.13: Employing a core for each query achieves limited I/O sharing due to the convoy phenomenon.

data multiple times. With this approach, only limited I/O sharing is achieved due to the convoy phenomenon.

An alternative approach is to have each processing core executing a separate table scan [127], as shown in Figure 2.14. In this case, a core is responsible for all queries but processes only a portion of the data; a given core feeds each block of tuples through every query before moving to the next block of tuples. In this case, the traditional division of work within the database is inverted. Instead of processing all the data blocks for an entire query at a time, each core processes a block of data at a time across all queries. So, the data is exploited as much as possible by keeping the tuples as long as possible in the caches.

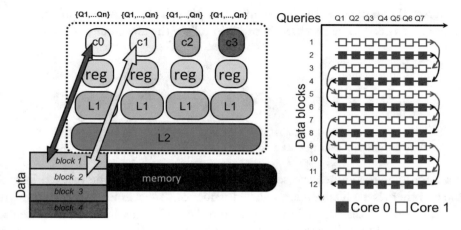

Figure 2.14: Employing a core for each table scan loads data into caches once and shares it, this way we reduce cache misses.

2.3.1 HORIZONTAL PARALLELISM IN ADVANCED DATABASE SCENARIOS

In this section, we show how two advanced database scenarios can benefit from horizontal parallelism. First, we study sorting, one of the most fundamental problems in database applications, in the context of multithreaded SIMD architecture. Then, we study how we can implement database cracking, an adaptive indexing method, in parallel mode. With both examples we expose that CPU-efficient algorithm implementation is not a simple task; on the contrary it requires proper study and design.

Horizontal parallelism in sorting

Here, we discuss in detail the example of sorting a list of numbers, combining and exploiting parallelization opportunities coming from two technologies discussed earlier, the SIMD and multicore capability of modern processors. Sorting is useful not only for ordering data, but also for other data operations, e.g., the creation of database indices, or binary search. In this section, we focus on how MergeSort can be optimized with the help of sorting networks and the bitonic merge kernel [32].

A sorting network, shown in Figure 2.15, is an abstract mathematical model that consists of a network of wires (parallel lines) and comparator modules (vertical lines). Each wire carries a value. The comparator connects two parallel wires and compares their values. It then sorts the values by outputting the smaller value to the wire at the top, and the larger value to the other wire at the bottom. In the first example, (on the left part of Figure 2.15), the top wire carries the value 2 and the bottom wire carries the value 5, so they will continue carrying the same values after the (vertical) comparator. In the second example (on the right part of Figure 2.15), the values on the wires need to be swapped in order to follow the aforementioned rule.

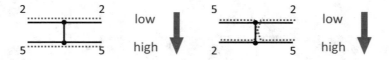

Figure 2.15: A rudimentary example of a sorting network.

In a bitonic merge kernel two sorted small sequences need to be merged in such a way that in the end there is a a blended large sorted sequence. An example is shown in Figure 2.16. Assume that sequence A is ordered in ascending order (A0 is the lower value of the sequence and A3 is the higher value of the sequence), and that sequence B is ordered in descending order. At the end, there is a sequence of N elements from Low to High (where $N = sizeof(A) + sizeof(B)$), where the lower value of the output sequence will be either A0 or B0 and the higher value will be either A3 or B3. To produce the ordered (blended) sequence one needs to make the shown comparisons represented as the vertical lines.

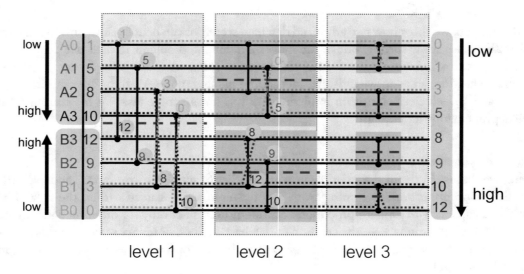

Figure 2.16: An example of a bitonic merge kernel.

Let us now see how the algorithm for the bitonic merge kernel works. In the example of Figure 2.16, with eight wires, there are three distinct levels. In the first level, the sorting network is split in half (denoted by the dashed line in the middle of level 1). Each input in the top half is compared to the corresponding input in the bottom half, i.e., the first wire in the first half is compared to the first wire in the second half, the second wire in the first half is compared to the second wire in the second half, etc., as shown in Figure 2.16. The dashed line in the first level produces two pieces wrapped in the two gray boxes in level 2, both the dashed lines and the gray boxes are used for illustration reasons only. In the second level, the same algorithm is applied in the two gray boxes and each piece from the previous level is split again in half. Each input in the top half of a piece is compared again to the corresponding input in the bottom half of the piece. In the third level, there are four pieces. In total, we need three levels to finally have a sorted sequence of numbers for the example of Figure 2.16. Bitonic mergesort is appropriate for SIMD implementation since the sequences of comparisons is known in advance, regardless of the outcome of previous comparisons. In this way, the independent comparisons can be implemented in a parallel fashion. The SIMD instructions required to produce the correct order at the end of each level are:

```
L1=SIMD_min(A,B);
H1=SIMD_max(A,B);
L1p=SIMD_shuffle(L1);
H1p=SIMD_shuffle(H1);
```

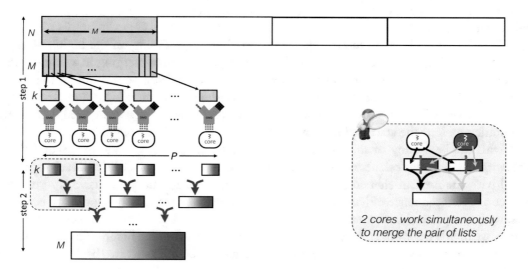

Figure 2.17: Sorting with multicore CPUs and SIMD instructions.

Now, let us see how the MergeSort algorithm is implemented [32]. Assume we have an array of N elements that we need to sort, as shown on top of Figure 2.17. The algorithm consists of two concrete phases. In *phase 1*, the array is evenly divided into chunks of size M, where M is such that the block can reside in the cache. Then, we need to sort each block (of size M) individually according to the following process. Each block is further divided into P pieces of size k, where k is the SIMD width, among the available hardware threads or CPU cores. Each thread sorts the data assigned to it by using an SIMD implementation of MergeSort. Merging networks are used to accomplish it. Merging networks expose the data-level parallelism that can be mapped onto the SIMD architecture. In Figure 2.17, we show the unsorted small pieces of input in light blue color and the corresponding sorted output as the gradient colored (from white to dark blue) small pieces. There is an explicit barrier at the end of the first step (i.e., sort), before the next step (i.e., merge) starts. At the end of the first step there are P sorted lists (as the number of CPU cores) of size k. In the second step of the first phase, we need to merge these sorted small lists to produce a single sorted list of size M. This requires multiple threads to work simultaneously to merge two lists. For example, for merging every two consecutive lists, we partition the work between two threads to efficiently utilize the available cores. Similarly, in the next iteration, four threads share the work of merging two sorted sequences. Finally, in the last iteration all available threads work together to merge the two lists and obtain the sorted sequence. At the end of the first phase, we have N/M sorted blocks, each of size M. In each iteration, we merge pairs of lists to obtain sorted sequences of twice the length than the previous iteration. Figure 2.17 depicts the phase 1 of the algorithm, as described above. In phase 2, we need to merge pairs of sorted lists of size M and finally produce the sorted list of the original whole input, list of size N. Again, all P processors work in parallel to merge the pairs of list in similar fashion as in phase 1.

Now let us see how we merge two small sorted arrays, focusing on the highlighted part on the right of Figure 2.17. One idea would be to assign the task of merging in a single thread. This solution, however, underutilizes the CPU, since the other core does nothing. Ideally, the two threads should collaborate (and work simultaneously) on the merging phase. To generate independent work for the threads, the median of the merged list is first computed [173]. This computation assigns the starting location for the second thread in the two lists. The first thread starts with the beginning of the two lists and generates k elements, while the second thread starts with the locations calculated above, and also generates k elements. Since the second thread started with the median element, the two generated lists are mutually exclusive, and together produce a sorted sequence of length 2k. Note that this scheme seamlessly handles all boundary cases, with any particular element being assigned to only one of the threads. By computing the median, we divide the work equally among the threads. Only when the first iteration finishes can the next one start. Now, in the next iteration, 4 threads cooperate to sort two lists, by computing the starting points in the two lists that correspond to the the 1/4th, 2/4th, and the 3/4th quantile, respectively.

In the above example, we show that the multithreaded SIMD implementation of the MergeSort algorithm requires careful tuning of the algorithm and the code, in order to properly exploit all the hardware features. In the following section, we will see in detail how another database scenario can be efficiently parallelized.

Horizontal parallelism in adaptive indexing

In this section, we discuss another advanced database scenario that takes advantage of horizontal parallelism. We show how adaptive indexing can be parallelized on multicore CPUs [111]. Database cracking [174] is the initial implementation of the adaptive indexing concept; there, the predicates of every range-selection query are used as pivots to physically partition the data in-place. Future queries on the same attribute further refine the index by partitioning the data. The resulting partitions contain only the qualifying data, so we see significant performance benefits on query processing over time (as queries arrive). Thus, the reorganization of the index is part of the query processing (i.e., of the select operator) using continuous physical reorganization.

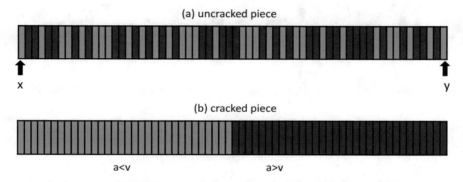

Figure 2.18: Database cracking

A visual example of the database cracking effect on the data is shown in Figure 2.18. Assume we pose the query SELECT max(a) FROM R WHERE a>v, In Figure 2.18(a), we show the original data (uncracked piece); pink indicates values that are lower than the pivot (value v) and blue indicates values that are greater than the pivot. The main idea is that two cursors, x and y, point at the first and at the last position of the piece, respectively. The cursors move toward each other, scanning the column, skipping values that are in the correct position while swapping wrongly located values. At the end of the query processing, values that are less or greater than the pivot finally lie in a contiguous space. Figure 2.19 shows the simplest partition & merge parallel implementation of database cracking. There, each thread works separately on a piece to produce a partially cracked piece. In our example, we show four threads that work separately and produce four partially cracked pieces. In each piece i we have two cursors x_i and y_i, at the first and the last position of the piece, that crack the piece as described in the single-threaded version of the algorithm above. Then, one thread needs to do the merging, and brings all the pink values to the front and all the blue values to the end of the array. During the merge phase the relocation of data causes many cache misses.

In [111], the authors propose a refined parallel partition & merge cracking algorithm that aims to minimize the cache misses of the merge phase. The new algorithm divides the uncracked

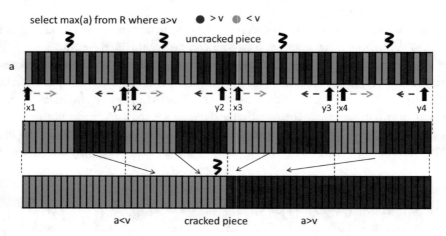

Figure 2.19: In parallel adaptive indexing, relocation during merge causes many cache misses.

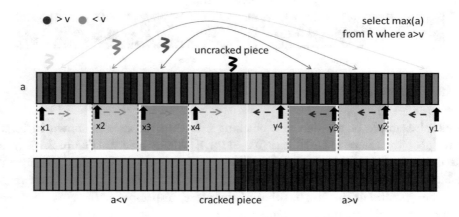

Figure 2.20: The refined version of parallel adaptive indexing moves less data during the merge phase.

piece into T partitions, as shown in Figure 2.20. The center partition is consecutive with size $S = \#elements/\#threads$, while the remaining T-1 partitions consist of two disjoint pieces that are arranged concentrically around the center partition. The authors make the assumption that the selectivity is known; it is expressed as a fraction of 1, the size of the left piece equals to $S * selectivity$, while the size of the right piece equals to $S * (1 - selectivity)$. In the example of Figure 2.20, the size of the disjoint pieces is equal, since the selectivity is 0.5 (50%). As in the simple partition & merge cracking, T threads crack the T partitions concurrently applying the original cracking algorithm. The thread that cracks the center (consecutive) partition swaps values within this partition. Although the refined algorithm (Figure 2.20) swaps values that are in longer distance compared to the simple algorithm (Figure 2.19), it moves less data during the merge phase because more data is already in the correct position. Both parallel algorithms make $O(n)$ comparisons/exchanges during the partitioning phase. However, the merging cost is significantly lower for the refined partition & merge cracking algorithm [111].

2.3.2   CONCLUSIONS

In summary, in this chapter we focused on improving the utilization of CPU resources. Going through the evolution of processor architecture, we discussed various parallelization opportunities within the CPU. Starting from the single-threaded architecture, we covered instruction- and data-level parallelism, and then we discussed SIMD, hyperthreading, and multithreaded implementations. Overall, CPU-tailored algorithm implementations require in-depth analysis and proper design in order to fully utilize the hardware. Naive implementations underutilize the hardware and show poor performance results. The next chapter focuses on the memory hierarchy and how software can be optimized to avoid memory stalls.

CHAPTER 3

Minimizing Memory Stalls

As Chapter 2 detailed, hardware vendors heavily innovated on implicit parallelism until 2005 through aggressive microarchitectural techniques (e.g., pipelining, superscalar execution, out-of-order execution, SIMD, etc.). Despite the differences across these techniques, all these innovations aim at one thing: minimizing the stall cycles where a core cannot retire an instruction. An instruction that completes all the five pipeline stages (described in Section 2.1) is *retired*. When an instruction gets stuck at one of the five pipeline stages, its execution is *stalled*. All the implicit parallelism techniques in modern hardware, become ineffective when an application exhibits excessive memory stalls. In other words, processor cannot retire instructions as efficiently as possible due to waiting for the instructions or data to be fetched from the memory hierarchy to be able to complete the five pipeline stages for those instructions.

The data management applications suffer from memory stalls in two ways: (1) memory access dependencies and (2) high data and instruction footprint. For example, during an index probe operation the next index node to be accessed depends on the index node that is currently accessed and the key value that is searched. In addition, the instruction and data footprints for data management applications usually exceed the size of the typical L1 caches.

To better understand this problem, Figure 3.1 shows the memory hierarchy of a typical server processor today. There are usually three levels of caches. The first-level caches are split between instructions and data, whereas the lower levels of the memory hierarchy are shared by instructions and data. The L1 instruction and data caches (32KB or 64KB) as well as the L2 caches (256KB) are private per core and the cores of a processor share the L3 or last-level cache (LLC) (10MB-40MB). While going down in this hierarchy, the access latencies drastically increase at each level. However, in practice, a superscalar core easily hides the latency of accessing the L1 caches. On the other hand, if a core cannot find a memory address in the L1 caches, then the lower levels of the memory should be searched. This might lead to stalls till the core gets the instructions or data needed to continue the execution. Such memory stalls are the dominant factor in the underutilization of a core's resources and have to be minimized.

3.1 WORKLOAD CHARACTERIZATION FOR TYPICAL DATA MANAGEMENT WORKLOADS

To understand the significance of the memory stalls for data management applications, there has been a large body of work characterizing the behavior of these applications on modern server hardware.

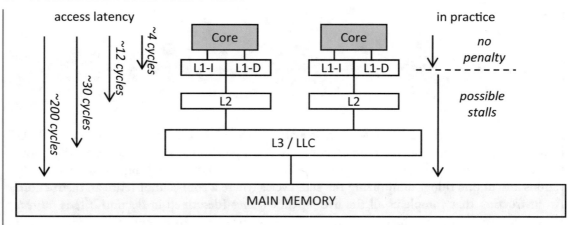

Figure 3.1: Memory hierarchy of commodity servers.

Barrosso et al. [16] investigate the memory system behavior of OLTP and DSS style workloads using TPC-B and TPC-D [155], respectively, both on a real machine and with a full-system simulation. They find that these two types of workloads need different architectural designs in terms of the memory system. Ranganathan et al. [132] use the same workloads as in [16]. However, they only focus on the effectiveness of out-of-order execution on SMPs while running these workloads in a simulation environment. Keeton et al. [75] experiment with TPC-C on a 4-way Pentium Pro SMP machine and perform a similar analysis to Barroso et al. [16] and Ranganathan et al. [132]. Stets et al. [145] perform a microarchitectural comparison between TPC-B [153] and TPC-C [154]. Ailamaki et al. [8] examine where the time goes on four different commercial DBMSs with a microbenchmark to have a finer-grain understanding of the memory system behavior of multiprocessors. All these studies conclude one main thing, data-intensive workloads cannot exploit aggressive microarchitectural features of modern processors very well, wasting most of their time in memory stalls and exhibiting low IPC.

More recent workload characterization studies [42, 141, 151, 152] highlight that this conclusion has not changed much today despite all the advancements in data management and hardware communities.

Figure 3.2 shows results from a workload characterization study for the applications that deal with big data management in the cloud, and, therefore, specifically designed to scale-out on modern servers [42]. The workload names from the corresponding benchmark suite, Cloud-Suite [33], are given on the x-axis. The first set of (gray) bars show the instructions retired per cycle (IPC) as these applications are run on an Intel server (Xeon X5670). Even though this server can actually retire up to four instructions in a cycle, it barely retires one when running these cloud applications. The red bars on the same graph highlight the main reason behind this underutilization in terms of IPC value. They show the % of the execution time that goes to memory stalls, and we clearly see that cores waste more than half of their execution cycles due to memory stalls for these workloads.

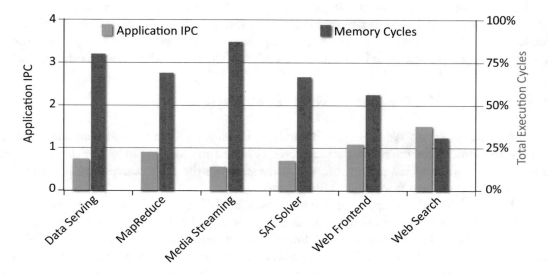

Figure 3.2: IPC and memory stalls in cloud workloads based on CloudSuite [33].

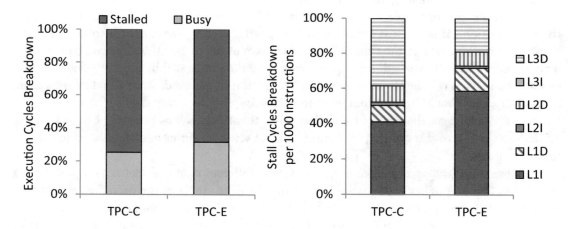

Figure 3.3: Execution and stall cycles breakdown for TPC-C and TPC-E benchmarks.

If we also look at the more traditional server workloads, Figure 3.3 has the breakdown of the execution and stall cycles when running the standardized OLTP benchmarks TPC-C [154] and TPC-E [156] in Shore-MT [68] on Intel server hardware (Xeon E5-2660) from the workload characterization studies of Tozun et al. [152]. While the graph on the left-hand side highlights the high stall time, the graph on the right-hand side demonstrates that this stall time is mainly due to the L1 instruction misses followed by the long-latency data misses from the last-level cache for traditional OLTP applications. In the case of instructions, the instruction footprint of transactions is simply too big to fit into a typical L1-I cache causing capacity misses, whereas for the data, the misses are compulsory as the data footprint of data intensive applications cannot possibly fit into any of the caches of the commodity server hardware [151].

3.2 ROADMAP FOR THIS CHAPTER

To sum up our problem: We have seen that today's fundamental data management applications heavily underutilize the microarchitectural resources of a core. More than half of the execution time goes to stalls, and the main sources of these stalls are the L1 instruction misses and the long-latency data misses from the last level cache.

It is unreasonable to expect the maximum possible IPC from data-intensive complex applications like data management systems since they tend to be memory bound. Fetching the necessary data and instructions from the lower levels of the memory hierarchy and exhibiting stalls and a low IPC value during this process is still useful work. However, there is room to improve the data and instruction access characteristics of various data management systems to reduce/minimize such stalls and achieve higher hardware utilization, system performance (higher throughput or lower latency), and energy-efficiency.

Even though the whole instruction footprint is much smaller than the data footprint for these applications, it is not small enough to fit in the L1 caches. We cannot increase the cache sizes, since it also increases the time to look for an item in the cache. Therefore, we need to find ways to reduce overall instruction footprint, minimize the jumps within the instruction stream, or give the illusion of a larger instruction cache. On the other hand, since the data misses are compulsory, one should instead find ways to only bring the necessary data cache lines[1] to the L1 data cache and get the best of them (i.e., reuse them as much as possible) before they are evicted. In the rest of this chapter, we are going to see several insights and techniques to achieve these two goals.

More specifically, first, Section 3.3 focuses on different data and instruction prefetching techniques that aim to bring the cache lines to the cache just prior to the time they are actually needed. This is mainly a hardware-side solution to our problem even though there are software-guided techniques for prefetching as well. Then, Section 3.4 surveys software-side attempts to make the applications more cache conscious. Finally, Section 3.5 advocates for more fine-grained task scheduling to maximize instruction cache locality.

---

[1]Cache line or cache block is the fixed-sized unit for content transfer between memory and the caches. On modern commodity hardware cache lines/blocks are typically 64bytes. In this book, we use cache lines and blocks interchangeably.

3.3   PREFETCHING

One of the well-studied techniques for improving instruction and data locality at various levels of the memory hierarchy is hardware prefetching. In this section, first, we go over the simpler prefetching techniques; which are the techniques we tend to see on modern processors because of their low algorithmic and space costs (Section 3.3.1). Then, we look at the temporal streaming which aims to exploit the recurring control flow in programs (Section 3.3.2). Finally, we conclude with software-guided prefetching techniques (Section 3.3.3).

3.3.1   TECHNIQUES THAT ARE COMMON IN MODERN HARDWARE

The most straightforward hardware prefetchers are the *stream prefetchers* [59]. Whenever there is a cache miss for an address, A, the prefetcher also fetches the next cache block of that address, A+1, A+2, ...The *next-line prefetcher* is a version of stream prefetcher, where only the next cache block, A+1, is fetched. How long these prefetchers wait before fetching the next addresses or how many next cache blocks they fetch changes from hardware to hardware or from instruction prefetchers to data prefetchers. However, in order to not to saturate the bandwidth or over-fill the cache with somewhat not useful content, stream prefetchers do not fetch more than three or four cache blocks.

The stream prefetchers basically favor sequential accesses. For instructions, this is in fact the case most of the time. Programs are naturally written that way. One doesn't have to pay too much extra attention to be able to exploit stream prefetching for instructions. However, there are branch statements or function calls in the code that might disrupt such sequentiality and leave stream prefetchers ineffective.

Compared to the instructions, the data accesses in an application might end up being all over the place unless the programmers pay close attention to the way they allocate and access the data. For example, many data management systems are written in a way to maximize sequential data access. This is traditionally done to exploit the sequential disk bandwidth through sequential scans. However, sequential scans are not just great for optimizing the accesses to disks, but also for memory accesses since they can exploit stream prefetchers that exists on modern hardware.

On the other hand, database operations like index lookups create pointer chasing problems. They are highly inefficient in terms of the data accesses as the data to be accessed next depends on what is accessed previously. Stream prefetchers fail to prevent cache misses due to these types of memory accesses.

Modern processors also offer other types of prefetchers—which are still not very complex even though they are more sophisticated than stream prefetchers—to cover the cases stream pretchers are not effective for. For instructions, the *branch predictors* predict the end result of branch conditions and possible function calls, and fetch the corresponding instructions just before they are needed. For the data, *stride prefetching* tries to handle cases where data is still accessed in an obvious order, but the order is not in such short distances as in stream prefetching. For example, after observing the misses of A and A+20, the stride prefetcher would fetch A+40 and A+60.

Even though these simpler prefetching techniques that exist on modern hardware help in reducing some of the instruction and data misses, they are not enough to minimize the memory stalls for memory-intensive applications like data management applications, as Section 3.1 summarized. It is not easy to tailor these simple prefetching techniques based on the needs of an application since the common wisdom is to take what is given from the hardware as is, and optimize software accordingly. The prefetching ideas presented in the next two subsections, on the other hand, target applications that have predictable data access behavior if one has a more detailed application-specific knowledge.

3.3.2   TEMPORAL STREAMING

Temporal streaming is a hardware prefetching technique based on the observation that most applications execute the same subset of actions over and over. As a result, in terms of their data and instruction accesses, they repeat similar or predictable trends in these actions. In the case of data management applications, these actions are database operations or sub-routines in database operations, as Section 3.5 will detail.

Figure 3.4 illustrates how temporal streaming works with an example using the index lookup operation in databases. As also mentioned in Section 3.3.1, an instance of the index lookup operation exhibits very irregular patterns in the way it accesses data and instructions. However, across different instantiations of this operation, the path or control flow that is followed does not change much. To start the search with a specific *key*, first, the *lookup* function would be called from the database API. Let's assume that this call brings two cache lines to the instruction cache, A and C. Then, *lookup* would call the *traverse* function to initiate an index tree traversal from root to leaves to find the *key*, which brings the cache lines X, Y, and Z to the cache. After *traverse* finishes, the program would go back to the *lookup* function, and execute the remaining logic of this function, bringing the cache lines C and D to the cache.

In this scenario, A, C, X, Y, Z, C, and D are called a *temporal stream*. *Temporal stream prefetchers* exploit this type of recurring control flow in various programs [43, 44, 74, 143]. If we keep a history of this routine, during the future instantiations of the index lookup operation, after observing the cache misses for A and C, we can fetch the cache lines X, Y, Z, and D.

Even though the example above focuses on instructions, similar temporal streams exist for data as well. For example, given an index identifier, the program has to access at least the metadata information for that index, the index root, and so on.

Prefetchers based on temporal streams can be much more accurate in terms of what they prefetch. The most state-of-the-art temporal streaming technique that we know of can give you up to 99% accuracy for instructions based on the hardware simulation results of Ferdman et al. [43] and Kaynak et al. [74]. However, these prefetchers need to do a lot of bookkeeping to keep a history of the temporal streams and identify them. The space overhead for very accurate

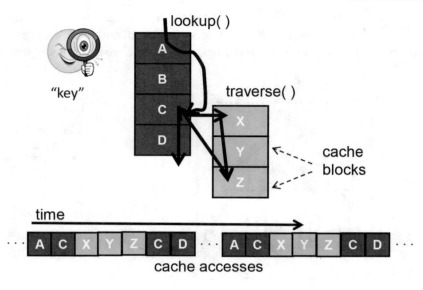

Figure 3.4: An example of temporal streaming [74].

prefetchers can be up to 40 KB per core [43], which is almost the L1 cache size on a modern processor, so it is hard to adopt temporal streaming on real hardware. There are recent proposals to reduce this space cost without losing the accuracy of the prefetching [74] by exploiting the code commonality across concurrent tasks (see also Section 3.5) in data management applications. Therefore, temporal streaming is still a promising technique. However, we are not aware of any modern architectures that adopt it yet.

3.3.3 SOFTWARE-GUIDED PREFETCHING

Section 3.3.2 describes a hardware-only technique that aims to exploit recurring control flows in programs, and highlights its overheads for the hardware. Can we instead exploit such recurring control flows without dumping all the cost to the hardware-side?

Software-guided prefetching can allow that at the cost of losing programmer-transparency. Rather than doing the bookkeeping at the hardware side to determine the recurring control flow, the programmers, who are actually aware of this control flow, can inject prefetching instructions where they think is necessary.

We can go over an example using the index lookup operation in databases once again, illustrated in Figure 3.5. When we start the search for a given key, we can first directly fetch the corresponding index root page as soon as the index lookup is called with a specific index identifier. Then while traversing the tree, we can prefetch the index nodes from the next level while processing the current level until we reach the index leaves [29, 98]. Similarly for the instructions, whenever we access the lookup function we can actually prefetch the instruction that corresponds to the function head for the traverse function, and leave the prefetching of the other instructions inside each function to the next-line prefetcher and branch predictor [10].

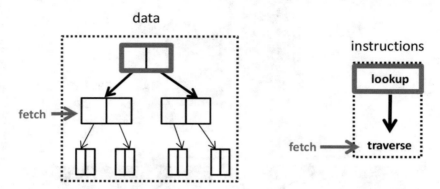

Figure 3.5: An example for software prefetching.

We need to be careful about how we utilize a software-guided prefetcher in practice, since we are giving the orders at the software side. We do not want to excessively prefetch everything in order to not to thrash the caches and saturate the bandwidth. There are hardware vendors that provide instructions for software-guided prefetching for data accesses only [1]. Even though this is not widely adopted in practice due to the difficulty of making optimal prefetching decisions, the software-guided data prefetching techniques mentioned in the above paragraph utilize these prefetch instructions provided by hardware at the software side.

3.4   BEING CACHE-CONSCIOUS WHILE WRITING SOFTWARE

While hardware offers some techniques to improve cache locality and utilization, one can also reduce cache misses and stalls by writing code in a more cache-conscious way. For example, reducing unnecessary complexity in systems, minimizing branch conditions in the code, or exploiting compilation optimizations might lead to fewer overall instructions and a smoother instruction stream (Section 3.4.1). In addition, designing data layouts that exhibit spatial locality would both utilize cache lines better be more friendly to hardware prefetchers (Section 3.4.2). Finally, changing execution models to enable instruction and data reuse could help significantly in reducing cache misses (Section 3.4.3).

3.4.1 CODE OPTIMIZATIONS

Writing Simpler Code

A way to optimize code is to write simpler code with fewer instructions. For example, the in-memory-optimized data management systems ([36, 146]) tend to have codebases that are written from scratch rather than adopting code from traditional systems. Furthermore, they do not have a buffer pool, which eliminates the code to executed for the buffer pool. Most of them depart from traditional row-level locking and adopt simpler locking mechanisms (as Section 4.1.1 details). Therefore, many other operations have a lot less code to execute as well. As a result, these systems exhibit smaller instruction footprints for the storage manager code, which increases the chances of having better cache locality.

Exploiting Modern Compilers

In addition to simplifying code and reducing the overall instruction footprint, better code compilation also aids in generating a more optimal instruction stream. For example, minimizing the jumps in the code would exploit the next-line prefetcher better. One can do this by either inlining the small frequently used functions or making sure that not so frequently taken branch conditions lay toward the end of the memory space allocated for the instructions of a function. This can be done either by a programmer writing code in a way that leads to a better instruction stream after compilation, or leaving it to the compilers to generate such code optimizations automatically. In practice, however, it is better to combine the the capabilities of the modern compilers with some minimal programmer effort. This way one does not reduce the programmer productivity much and can exploit more compilation optimizations.

One way to utilize compilation optimizations is to use profile-guided optimizations [2]. If you are a data management system vendor and can access a sample version of a customer's workload, then you can profile your code by running this workload on your system. Based on this profiling the compiler would generate a more optimized code for the workload at hand. This, of course, is a static approach; meaning that if you want to change your workload, you would probably want to re-do the profiling and generate new optimized code.

It is also possible to perform compilation optimizations dynamically at runtime so that if your workload changes you can adapt at run time. Changing code layout at runtime has its own overheads, and might cause unpredictability in terms of overall performance. The improvements introduced by modern JVMs (e.g., HotSpot VM [6]) in doing just-in-time (JIT) compilation, however, has been increasing the adoption and success of this approach in recent years.

Custom Code Generation

Finally, both academia [7, 86, 102] and industry [4, 46, 160] have been paying attention to developing custom code generation/compilation mechanisms to allow just-in-time compilation of queries at runtime to achieve more optimal code and data processing paths for specific queries. For example, HyPer [102] does this to minimize the overheads associated with traditional interpreted languages, and optimize data cache access. As a side-effect, it highly improves the instruction cache accesses as well. Microsoft's Hekaton [46] compile the stored procedures into machine code to get rid of the overhead of SQL compilation and generate more optimized instructions for those stored procedures. The wide-adoption and success of this approach today shows that it is a powerful mechanism to optimize memory accesses of a data management system.

name	color
erietta	blue
pinar	red
danica	green
iraklis	orange

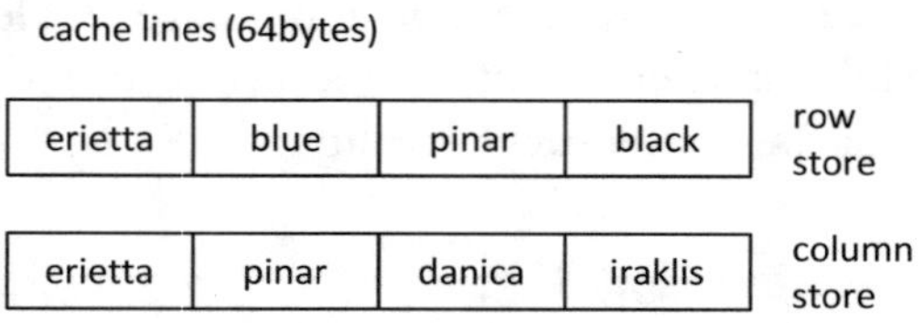

Figure 3.6: Row-wise vs columnar data layouts.

3.4.2 DATA LAYOUTS

After seeing how to achieve more cache-friendly code layouts, this section highlights the key insights for optimizing data layouts. Deciding on the most optimal data layout depends highly on the data access patterns of a program.

Data Pages

Figure 3.6 shows a table with two columns on the left-hand side: the first column is the name of the people in this database and the second column is a color associated with the person. Let's assume that each column is 16 bytes in this example. Therefore, any 4 of these columns can fit in one cache line considering that most processors have 64 bytes cache lines. Modern data management systems have two major ways of storing these columns inside the database pages. The first one is the *row-wise* approach where the rows are stored one after the other in database pages. When this table is accessed, the data brought into the cache line would probably look like the example at the top in the right-hand side of Figure 3.6. The second one is the *column-wise* approach where the values that belong to a column are stored together in a database page. The bottom example in the right-hand side of Figure 3.6 illustrate how the cache lines would be when this table is accessed in the case of columnar layout.

These different data layouts for databases mainly stem from optimizing for the disk accesses, but their key insights are also applicable to accesses to main-memory. For a particular application, one should pick the data layout that would maximize the usage of the data brought into the cache and exploit the simple next-line prefetching. For example, the OLTP workloads tend to read several columns from the table when they access a record. Therefore, it's better to use a row store so that one can utilize more of the cache line brought into the cache. If you want to read the whole record for texttterietta, under columnar format, one would bring an additional cache-line into the cache (in addition to the one shown in Figure 3.6). On the other hand, the OLAP workloads perform longer scan operations over a few columns. Therefore, having the values from a column stored close to each other helps—in terms of both cache line utilization and exploiting the next-line prefetcher.

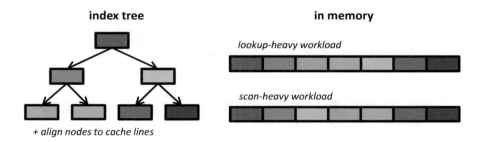

Figure 3.7: Cache-conscious index layouts.

Index Pages

One can do similar trade-offs for index pages. Figure 3.7 shows an high-level representation of an index at the left-hand side. In order to determine the best way to arrange the layout for the individual index nodes, we again need to know the characteristics of accesses to this index. There is not one layout that works perfectly for all types of workloads. For example, the workload is more lookup-heavy or a pattern mining workload, the layout shown at the top on the right-hand side of Figure 3.7 where the pages for the index nodes are allocated one after the other in a depth-first order would perform better in terms of data locality. On the other hand, for a workload that performs frequent index scans, arranging index nodes in a breadth-first order (Figure 3.7 bottom right-hand side) would achieve better data locality. In addition, for mostly in-memory accesses arranging the size of the index nodes to match the cache line size or some multiple of the cache-line size gives benefits.

3.4.3 CHANGING EXECUTION MODELS

In addition to improving the code and data layouts, we can also change some of our core execution mechanisms and algorithms.

Traditionally, databases adopt the volcano iterator model where each database operator has the interface shown in Figure 3.8(a). Each operator has a `next` function call to get the next tuple to process. For example, when the scan operator starts to scan a column of a table from the beginning to end, it is going to retrieve the first value (`erietta`) for the scanned column. Then, the select operator is going to ask for the next column value to process from the scan

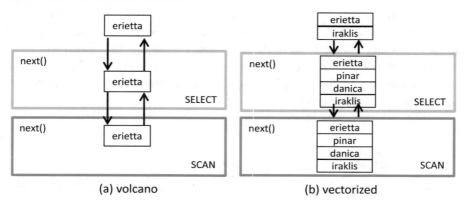

(a) volcano   (b) vectorized

Figure 3.8: Volcano vs. vectorized execution models.

operator, which moves the current column value to the next operator. If the current column value satisfies the query condition, it is going to be in the output. Therefore, with this execution model processes elements tuple-at-a-time from the first operator to the last. This leads to poor locality in terms of both data and instruction accesses. In the case of data, even though there is locality for the one tuple/column being processed, the locality for the state information kept at each operator is lost. Similarly for instructions, one needs to load the instructions for each stage one after the other for each tuple/column being processed, thus, exhibiting poor code reuse and locality.

Vectorized execution (Figure 3.8(b)) proposes the following to overcome the sub-optimal characteristics of the volcano-style execution model. Rather than processing tuples/columns one at a time, operators would process a vector of tuples or columns at a time. When every next operator asks for more tuples/columns, a vector of values that satisfy the conditions of the current operator is sent to the next one. This execution model improves data locality since it enables re-use for the state information data kept at each operator. It also improves instruction locality since the instructions for each operator would be re-used for the vector of columns. In addition to improving cache locality, vectorized execution also helps in terms of exploiting techniques like SIMD since one can feed this vector to your SIMD instructions.

To sum up: for being cache conscious one can do two orthogonal things: (1) improving the layout and footprint of your code and data, and (2) developing alternative execution models that are more aware of the underlying memory hierarchy. Following from alternative execution models, the next section illustrates alternative ways of scheduling big tasks that are formed of several smaller actions from a pre-defined set. The goal of this would be to exploit the common instructions across these tasks to maximize instruction locality. In the context of databases, these tasks would be transactions and queries while the small actions would be database operations.

3.5 EXPLOITING COMMON INSTRUCTIONS

Transactions are composed of *actions* that in turn may execute several basic functions. Basic function examples include probing and scanning an index, inserting a tuple to a table, updating a tuple, etc. No matter how different the output or high-level functionality of one transaction are from another, all database transactions contain such common basic functions [150].

This section describes three ways of scheduling similar transactions: the conventional way and the two techniques (academic proposals) that exploit instruction commonality across transactions.

Conventional/Traditional transaction scheduling

Figure 3.9a and Figure 3.9c show how three transactions executing exactly the same code parts would execute under a conventional OLTP system on one core and on multiple cores, respectively. The example transactions execute the code segments A, B, and C in order. Each segment fits in L1-I, but any two segments exceed its capacity. When these transactions execute in a conventional system, they take turns thrashing the cache since each executes segments A–C in order independent of the other transactions. Thus, each segment incurs an overhead due to instruction cache misses.

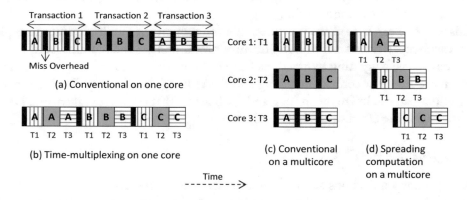

Figure 3.9: Ways of scheduling transactions.

Transactions time-multiplexing on a single core

Figure 3.9b shows a way of improving L1-I utilization when transactions are running on a single core. The first, *lead*, transaction executes segment A incurring an overhead as in the case of conventional scheduling. However, instead of proceeding to execute segment B, transaction 1 context switches allowing, in turn, transactions 2 and 3 to execute instead. Transactions 2 and 3 find segment A in L1-I and thus incur no overhead due to misses. Once all three transactions execute the first segment, execution proceeds to segment B, and so on.

This way transactions time-multiplex on a core in a way that would maximize their instruction cache locality. The more frequent context switching for transactions comes at a cost. This cost of context switching, however, can be minimized by either adopting a hardware-side approach (e.g., STREX [14]) or implementing a more specialized context switching method at the software-side (STEPS [55]). The more frequent context switching can also potentially hinder data locality for transactions and increase the transaction latency. However, the overall throughput benefits from this way of scheduling because of the increased instruction cache locality. In certain cases, this way of scheduling even benefits data cache locality, especially at the levels of the cache hierarchy that are above L1-D, if transactions access common read-only data.

Spreading computation of a transaction
As long as there are enough cores so that the aggregate L1-I capacity can hold all code segments, a transaction can migrate to the core whose L1-I cache holds the code segment the transaction is about to execute. For example, as Figure 3.9d shows, the *lead* transaction can execute segment A first on core 1, then migrate to core 2 where it would execute segment B, then migrate to core 3 where it would execute segment C. Transactions 2 and 3 can follow in a pipelined fashion, finding segments A, B, and C, in cores 1, 2, and 3, respectively. While transaction 1 incurs an overhead when fetching the segments for the first time (as in the case of the previous mechanism), the other transactions do not.

This way one can spread the execution of a transaction over multiple cores to exploit the aggregate cache capacity that exists on multicore hardware and the code commonality across concurrent transactions. Migrating transactions from one core to another of course has some drawbacks: the more frequent context switching and the reduced data locality. Enabling hardware-level migrations can minimize the former, and the benefits that come from increased L1-I cache locality overweigh the effect of the latter [13, 26, 150].

3.6 CONCLUSIONS

Data management applications severely underutilize a core's resources since they exhibit high memory stall times. We have seen that the main reasons for these memory stalls are the L1-level instruction cache misses and the long latency data misses from the last level cache. Keep in mind that the overall instruction footprint for main data management applications are much smaller than the data footprint. However, they still don't fit in the first-level caches and this is a problem and we cannot just increase L1 cache sizes since it also increases the time to look for an item in the cache. Current prefetching techniques help but are not enough; we need to find ways to both reduce instruction footprint and also somewhat give the illusion of a larger L1 cache capacity without actually increasing the L1 cache sizes. On the other hand, the data footprint for the data-intensive applications are too big to maintain a perfect cache locality. Data misses are inevitable and data re-use is also quite low as we have seen in one of the previous graphs. The important thing here is to make the best use of the cache-lines brought into the cache, avoiding cases where only a small portion of the whole cache line is used. Picking the right layout for the application at hand is a crucial step in achieving better cache line reuse and exploiting existing hardware prefetchers.

PART II

Explicit/Horizontal Scalability

CHAPTER 4

Scaling-up OLTP

Different types of workloads are subjecting the database management systems to different kinds of scalability challenges. For transaction processing systems where many threads access small portions of the data and enter numerous critical sections to ensure ACID properties, the main challenge that limits scalability is the access latency to the shared data items in other cores' caches.

We illustrate the scalability challenges by reviewing the life of a transaction in a traditional centralized transaction processing system that uses pessimistic 2-phase locking (2PL) and write-ahead logging. When such a system is deployed on a multicore system, it typically has a thread pool comprised of a number of threads that run on different cores in a system. When a transaction arrives in the system, it is assigned to the available thread that completes all operations requested by a transaction or queued to the input queue if all threads are busy. Each thread accesses all data items requested by a transaction. Before doing so, it has to obtain locks from the centralized lock manager. Once it is granted a lock on a particular data item, it needs to also obtain latches that protect physical data before accessing it. If it has performed any changes, it needs to log them which requires obtaining space in the log buffer and writing the log to the stable storage. Finally, it has to update the metadata—the data structures that store the systems state to ensure correctness of transaction execution. Thus, it is not surprising that a typical transaction accesses many shared data structures in the critical path which requires a lot of synchronization and poses significant scalability challenges [67].

To illustrate the necessity of synchronization, in Figure 4.1 we plot the data access patterns by tracing accesses of individual threads to different records of the DISTRICT table over one second while running TPC-C workload. Each thread is assigned a different color and each dot represents a single access. We observe from this graph that there is no predictability in data accesses between threads and records. Hence, in order to ensure transactional (ACID) properties, the system needs to enter numerous critical sections.

We break down the critical sections entered by Shore-MT when executing a single transaction that updates one row in Figure 4.2. The locking component alone accounts for over 20 critical sections with a similar number of critical sections related to latching and metadata accesses. Logging is another bottleneck in the system partly because of the number of critical sections and partly because of the length of critical sections involved in long latency I/O operations that increase contention.

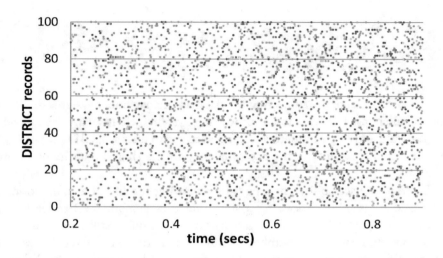

Figure 4.1: Data access patterns on the **District** table when running TPC-C benchmark.

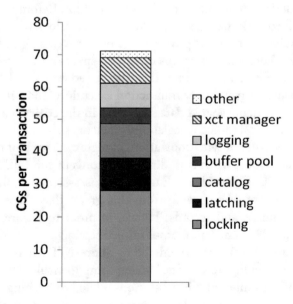

Figure 4.2: Breakdown of critical section by component on Shore-MT running the transaction that updates one record.

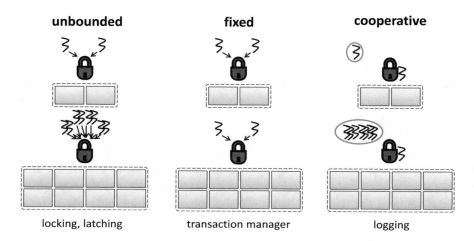

Figure 4.3: Scalability behavior of different types of critical sections as the number of threads in a system increases.

In general, critical sections can be classified into three groups: unbounded, fixed, and cooperative [67] whose scalability behavior we depict in Figure 4.3. **Unbounded** critical sections are the ones where all threads have to access a centralized synchronization point. These critical sections are the main scalability bottleneck with an increasing number of threads in the system, as even the shortest critical section can become a major bottleneck. Many unbounded critical sections can be found in traditional locking and latching components of the system. **Fixed** critical sections are the ones where there is a fixed number of threads entering them regardless of the number of threads in the system. These are good critical sections as they will not become a bottleneck with more threads. Typical examples are producer consumer pairs that can be found in the transaction manager. **Cooperative** critical sections are the ones where different threads can combine their requests while waiting to enter a critical section. These are also good as they do not create additional contention. They are utilized in logging approaches such as Aether [69] where multiple threads can batch their log buffer insert requests. In general, to achieve scalability in the face of increasing number of threads, one needs to either eliminate unbounded communication or turn them into fixed or cooperative ones which do not cause scalability bottlenecks.

In the rest of this section, we specifically examine scalability challenges related to locking, latching, and logging components of the system. For each one of them we survey the representative approaches to overcoming the challenges. Next, we provide a brief overview of the synchronization mechanisms that are essential to achieving scalability on multicores. Finally, we outline the challenges posed by the non-uniformity of communication latencies on OLTP systems and survey the approaches to overcome them before concluding.

4.1 FOCUS ON UNSCALABLE COMPONENTS

4.1.1 LOCKING

To better understand the sources of unscalable behavior of a traditional lock manager when using 2PL protocol, we examine the typical interaction pattern between the lock manager and a worker thread executing a transaction. At the beginning of a transaction, the thread first requests all the locks it needs, before proceeding to perform the operation on the locked data. After completing the execution and deciding to commit, or, in case of errors, abort the transaction, it releases all locks and finishes the transaction. This process repeats for the next transaction and the third transaction and so on. It is the same for both hot and cold locks, as illustrated in Figure 4.4. The hot locks are the ones that are acquired and released repeatedly and they comprise metadata locks on the schema of the data and its top-level elements—tables and root nodes of B-trees. However, as most accesses are directed to individual rows, most of these locks are shared or intention shared locks that are granted in almost all cases.

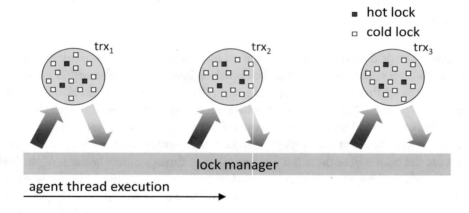

Figure 4.4: Locking patterns in a typical OLTP system.

One way of reducing physical contention on the lock manager is to decrease the number of interactions per transaction. The main idea of speculative lock inheritance is to allow the next transaction to inherit hot locks instead of repeatedly releasing and acquiring the same set of locks [66]. It works as follows: at commit time, a transaction doesn't release all locks. Instead, it releases cold locks and saves hot locks. When the next transaction comes in, it inherits the saved locks and releases the ones it does not need. By reducing the number of lock requests, this technique significantly reduces contention in the lock manager, especially for the read-only workloads.

Another approach that achieves the same effect are the lightweight intent locks (LIL) [82]. LIL technique is based on the observation that intent locks are the hottest locks in the system. Additionally, their number is fairly small which causes high contention. To relieve this

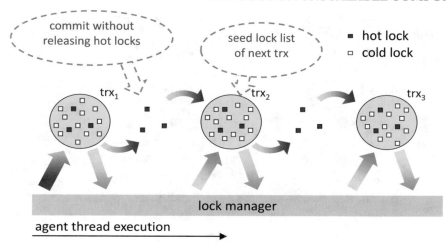

Figure 4.5: Speculative lock inheritance.

contention, LIL implements intent locks as counters directly in the data pages, so threads acquire and release them without the need to access the lock manager. These operations are performed using atomic compare-and-swap instructions.

While these two techniques help alleviate the contention on the lock manager, they do not eliminate it completely. One way to increase scalability of the lock manager, without changing the concurrency control protocol used, is to partition the data and distribute the lock manager.

Data-oriented transaction execution (DORA) model divides the database into logical partitions [108]. Each transaction is broken into smaller requests—actions, and each action is executed by a thread that has exclusive access to the partition where the data accessed by the action resides. With this mechanism, the lock manager is distributed and lock manager interaction is localized within a single core. Figure 4.6 illustrates the access pattern of DORA for the same workload as in Figure 4.1. The predictable access pattern eliminates most of the locking-related synchronization and improves scalability.

While logical partitioning alleviates locking bottleneck, it does not tackle other bottlenecks. Hence, using a different system architecture is an appealing way to eliminate multiple scalability bottlenecks at once and avoid challenges posed by multicores. Recently, there has been a wave of fine-grained shared nothing systems that take partitioning to the extreme. They typically partition the data completely and execute transaction on the partitions in the single-threaded fashion. In this way, they do not need any locking or latching. Also, they are optimized for today's large main memories and typically do not have a buffer pool. However, they do support persistence on disk, typically through asynchronous checkpointing. Finally, as traditional ARIES-style physiological logging poses too many overheads, these systems provide durability either through replication or using lightweight form of logical logging [97]. In general, they are

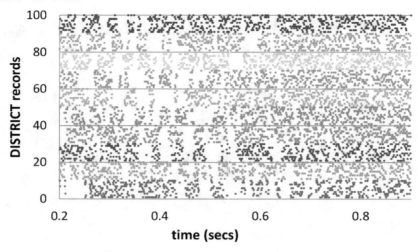

Figure 4.6: Data-oriented execution makes access patterns predictable and improves locality.

optimized for predefined set of transaction types that are compiled ahead of time [146, 147]. Shared-nothing systems are ideal for perfectly partitionable workloads where a single transaction accessed only data from its local partition. However, in many workloads this is not the case because they are not easy to partition without causing many multisite transactions or heavy skew. Multisite transactions, especially ones that access large portion of data, present a significant challenge.

We briefly survey representative systems and outline their main characteristics and different approaches they take to address the challenge. H-Store and its commercial version VoltDB take the extreme approach with single-threaded processes and durability achieved by replication [146]. This design allows them to scale well for perfectly partitionable In the initial design, multisite transactions were executed with two phase commit protocol with up to two network roundtrips which caused low concurrency even with few multisite transactions. Speculative optimistic concurrency control allows local transactions to proceed speculatively while the node is waiting for the network reply. However, they need to verify their results before committing [70].

HyPer is a system that support both OLTP and OLAP [76]. It also uses single-threaded execution model and relies on compilation of transaction plans that generate long pipelines optimized for data locality [102]. This approach minimizes branching in code to achieve very good cache efficiency and high single-thread throughput. They support OLAP queries through copy-on-write mechanisms that utilize virtual memory. Initially, multisite transactions required all threads in the system to execute a single multisite transaction at a time. Recently, there were proposals to (1) increase concurrency of general transactions using optimistic concurrency control (OCC) with strict timestamp ordering, (2) optimize execution of long-running transactions by splitting them into read-only and update sub-transactions with tentative execution, (3) multiplex transaction with MVCC on a single thread, and (4) use hardware transaction memory to implicitly lock data items [92, 101, 103, 165].

Finally, Calvin is a recent system that proposes using deterministic execution model to achieve high throughput even when a system is running across different datacenters [148, 149]. The main idea is to first perform centralized dependency detection to eliminate any need for coordination at commit time. Transactions are assigned to a partition where they first acquire all necessary locks and then proceed to execute the whole transaction possibly involving remote reads. Initially, locks were acquired through traditional lock manager, but an improved proposal argues for the use of very lightweight locking (VLL) scheme that collocates locks with data records and performs selective contention analysis to determine which of the waiting threads will be granted the lock upon release [133].

While partitioning-based approaches can achieve scalability for workloads that are amenable to partitioning, improving scalability of all concurrency control schemes on multicores is beneficial for workloads that cannot be easily partitioned. Serializable snapshot isolation (SSI) is another way to ensure isolation between concurrent transactions. It typically includes a validation phase during transaction commit [41]. Main techniques that can be used to achieve scalability of SSI on multicores include memory-friendly validation phase without read after write conflicts and the use of bulk memory operations whenever possible [71].

A standard 2PL scheme poses significant overhead for systems optimized for main memory. These systems typically use optimistic concurrency control techniques that are implemented lock-free. One example is the scheme used in Microsoft's Hekaton main-memory system [36, 89]. Transactions track their begin and end timestamps and validate read and scan sets during the commit processing step. To support non-blocking nature of transaction processing in Hekaton, transactions that read data written by transaction in the commit phase and take a commit dependency on it. The idea of lock-free OCC for main-memory databases is taken a step further in Silo which decentralized the timestamp allocator to remove any centralized data structure in Hekaton's scheme [158]. While many subsequent proposals enhance OCC or 2PL schemes for multicores [38, 79, 81, 169, 170], a recent study has shown that none of the proposals effectively scale to 1,000 cores [168].

4.1.2   LATCHING

While the lock manager arbitrates data access at the logical level, latching the individual pages, that contain the accessed data, does so at the physical level. Physical contention is especially acute when the tables are accessed through the primary key index implemented as a B-tree. In that case, all thread accessing data in a particular table have to acquire latches on the same set of pages on the upper levels of the tree, leading to high contention. Even if the data is logically partitioned, i.e., as in the data-oriented execution model.

As the next step after logical partitioning utilized by the DORA system is the partitioning at the physical layer, achieved by replacing the single rooted B-tree structure with a multirooted one and ensure that the ranges of each subtree would match the partition ranges of the logical partitioning [109]. In this multirooted B-tree structure, the new tree root becomes a routing table which keeps the information on which range corresponds to which subtree so that it can route the worker threads to the correct subtree. And as a result of this partitioning, index pages can be accessed latch-free. By forcing a heap page to be pointed by only one leaf page, one also achieves single-threaded access to each heap page and eliminate latching from heap pages as well. Also, with this design each thread can effectively cache their metadata information since they keep accessing the same tables so contention on catalog manager can also be eliminated.

A way to remove latching bottleneck without data partitioning is to redesign the B-tree itself to support latch-free operations. PALM is one proposal for designing latch-free concurrent B-tree [139]. It requires the threads that access the B-tree to proceed in lockstep up and down the tree and to synchronize between phases. Each thread is executing a batch of operations on a range of keys with reads proceeding before modifications. This allows them to avoid global barriers and requires threads to synchronize only with a couple of neighboring threads. At each step only one thread is allowed to modify any particular node. To achieve good efficiency without sacrificing latency, PALM uses software prefetching for nodes on the next level and SIMD to accelerate operations on each level.

BW-tree is another latch-free B-tree which is optimized for both main memory and flash [93]. It is log structured which maximizes the number of sequential writes. Data is organized into elastic-sized pages and accessed through the PIDs stored in the mapping table. Mapping tables map page IDs (PIDs) to both locations in the main memory and on the stable storage. BW-tree pages are not updated in place. Instead, delta updates are prepended to the page and their pointers are updated atomically in the mapping table which improves cache behavior. Updates are periodically installed into consolidated pages. In general, structure modifying operations (SMOs) are done in a series of atomic steps by different threads in an opportunistic fashion—if a thread wants to access the page in the middle of a SMO, it first completes the SMO.

4.1.3   LOGGING

Traditional write-ahead logging (WAL) scheme is vulnerable to multiple sources of contention that we illustrate in Figure 4.7 through discussion of thread's interaction with the log manager. During the execution, whenever a transaction wants to perform a data modification (insert, update, or delete), it first acquires required locks, performs the modification, and then logs the changes by writing the log record to the log buffer. After all the changes are completed and the transaction is ready to commit, it flushes all the changes performed by a transaction to the stable storage for durability. After the changes are durable, transaction releases all locks and completes the commit.

Figure 4.7 illustrates three major contention serialization points:

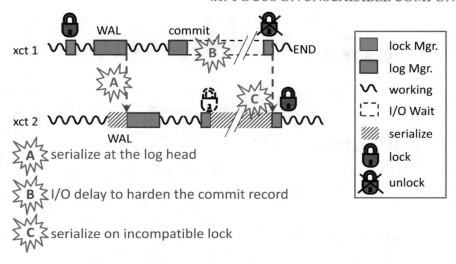

Figure 4.7: Sources of contention in log manager.

- when a thread wants to insert a new log record, it needs to acquire space in the centralized log buffer and write the generated record;

- at commit time, making log records durable incurs long I/O delays due to both the latency of writing to the stable storage (typically HDD or SSD) and the overhead of system calls; and

- since locks are held until log records become durable, they potentially significantly increase contention on the locks for frequently updated data items.

Aether tackles these problems in a holistic fashion by combining three techniques, illustrated in Figure 4.8 [69]. First, early lock release allows transactions to release shared locks at the beginning of the commit phase before the log buffer is persisted. Controlled lock violation takes this a step further by allowing an exclusive lock to also be released by tracking dependencies until the transaction commit finishes [51]. Flush pipelining reduces context switches and I/O delay by delegating log flushing to a dedicated thread in a fashion similar to group commit. Contrary to group commit, it does not violate the durability requirement because the results are returned to the user only after the transaction becomes durable. Consolidation array is a technique that exemplifies conversion of a fixed to composable critical section. Instead of all threads contending to inserting data into the log buffer, waiting threads combine their requests for log buffer space and can insert their log records in parallel once they get that space.

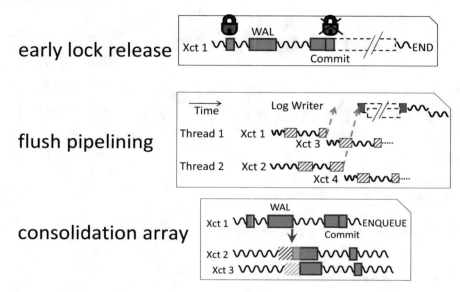

Figure 4.8: Aether applies different techniques to alleviate contention.

4.1.4   SYNCHRONIZATION

While the three components we examined in more detail in the previous subsections require a substantial number of critical sections, other components also have many synchronization points. Accesses to all of these critical sections are spread out during the execution of a transaction and they have different durations and access patterns. As there are many ways to implement a critical section, the important question is which synchronization primitive is best for each case. Next, we give a brief overview of typical lock-based and lock-free approaches.

OS mutex is the simplest way to implement a critical section and is available from standard compiler libraries. However, it requires system calls which pose non-negligible overhead and do not scale with contention. Test and set spinlocks are efficient due to their simplicity, but they do not scale with contention. Queue-based spinlocks, such as MCS spinlocks, are scalable, however they require more complex memory management. Finally, reader-writer locks permit concurrent readers, however they pose higher overhead than write-only locks.

On the lock-free side, atomic operations are very efficient as they are implemented with hardware instructions, however they are limited to updates to a single value. Lock-free algorithms can be scalable, but each case requires a special purpose algorithm. OCC is another appealing approach that has low overhead for reads, but contending writes can cause livelock.

4.2   NON-UNIFORM COMMUNICATION

Multisocket multicore systems are the predominant configuration for database servers today and are expected to remain popular in the future. The non-uniformity of such systems impacts communication between cores as well as between cores and memory. Here we focus on inter-core communication as it has bigger impact on OLTP, while the non-uniformity in memory accesses is discussed in more details in Section 5.2. Figure 4.9 shows a simplified diagram of a typical machine that has two sockets with quad-core CPUs. Communication between the numerous cores happens through different mechanisms. For example, two threads running on the same core can communicate very fast through the core's L1 cache. When they're running on different cores on the same socket, they communicate through the socket's last-level (L3) cache. Finally, two threads running on different sockets need to use inter-socket links. Therefore, depending on the thread placement, communication latencies can vary by an order of magnitude. In this environment we identify Islands as groups of cores that communicate much faster among themselves than with cores from other groups.

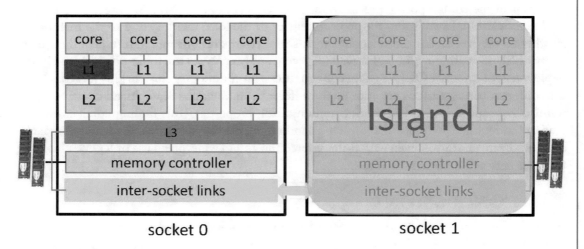

Figure 4.9: A schematic view of a multisocket multicore server. We identify a hardware *Island*: a group of cores that communicate faster with each other than with the cores from another island.

It might be appealing to consider a server with multiple islands as a distributed system and deploy shared-nothing systems on it. A recent study compares a range of different distributed deployment configurations from shared-everything to fine-grained shared-nothing including Island shared-nothing that deploys one database instance on each Island [116]. This study concludes that at one extreme shared-nothing offers stable performance in the presence of multisite transactions, but it is rarely optimal. On the other hand, shared-nothing offers fast performance for perfectly partitionable workloads but it's sensitive to skew and distributed transactions. Island shared-nothing offers robust middle ground. The main takeaways is that optimal configuration depends on the combination of hardware and workload characteristics. When any one of these characteristics change, a system needs to adapt to the new best configuration which is expensive due to the need to move data between different processes.

ATraPos solves this problem by making a shared-everything system scalable on Islands and adaptive to any changes in the workload characteristics or hardware topology [115]. It relies on precise data partitioning and placement to maximize locality of data accesses and on adaptive repartitioning to maintain data locality even when the workload changes. ATraPos ensures stable performance by choosing the appropriate partitioning scheme, which maximizes resource utilization and balances the load. The choice is based on a cost model that takes into account (a) the static data dependencies, (b) the dynamic workload information, and (c) the underlying hardware topology. Finally, ATraPos uses a lightweight monitoring mechanism to continuously track the transaction behavior. When it detects that the workload has changed, it adjusts the data partitioning and partition placement to guarantee high and predictable performance.

As the number of cores on a chip increases, multiple Islands are forming within a single processor in the contemporary processors such as Oracle SPARC M7, AMD EPYC, and Intel Xeon Scalable. In addition, the access latencies to the local memory and to the memory of another server over fast interconnect in a rack-scale system are converging, thus creating a hierarchy of Islands within a group of servers. A recent study analyzes the trade-offs involved in the deployment of different OLTP system configurations on commodity clusters [117]. It concludes that different configurations are optimal for different combinations of workload characteristics, multisocket topologies, and network communication properties. This finding emphasizes that scaling out requires both Island and inter-Island awareness to efficiently utilize emerging rack-scale hardware platforms, even with faster interconnects and widespread use of RDMA blurring the lines between different machines.

4.3   CONCLUSIONS

Increasing numbers of processor cores found in modern multicores and non-uniformity in multisocket system pose significant challenges to scalability of transaction processing systems. In order to overcome scalability challenges, system designers can take one of the two principal approaches:

- take the existing system, identify scalability bottlenecks and remove them in a holistic fashion without creating any new bottlenecks; or

- start from scratch and design scalable systems for multicores. The most important lesson in this case is to not repeat old mistakes.

One of the concerns which will only become more significant is the non-uniformity in communication, so systems need to optimize for locality of communication. Also, they need to make systematic decisions about the optimal synchronization mechanism for each critical section.

CHAPTER 5

Scaling-up OLAP Workloads

In the previous chapter, we showed that scaling-up OLTP workloads on modern hardware is sensitive mostly to the latency of memory accesses. In this chapter, we show that scaling-up OLAP workloads involves further challenges that pertain to the efficient utilization and saturation of the limited number of hardware resources, e.g., the number of hardware contexts and the memory bandwidth.

Figure 5.1 shows the two major challenges we focus on in this chapter. The first challenge involves redundant computations. As more and more hardware contexts are supported on modern hardware, an increasing number of concurrent queries can be evaluated. As concurrency increases, there may be sharing opportunities among the queries. Conventional execution engines in DBMS do not exploit these sharing opportunities. By sharing across queries, DBMS can decrease contention for resources significantly by avoiding redundant operations. In Figure 5.1a, we see an example of an analytical workload, where queries have similar parts. After the number of concurrent queries surpasses the number of available hardware contexts, and the

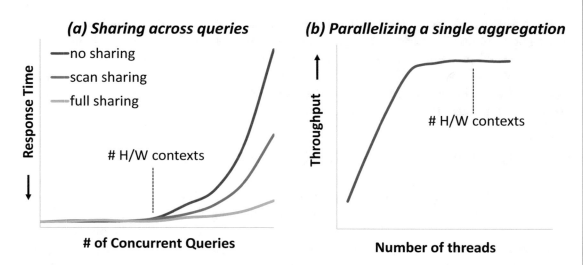

Figure 5.1: (a) Scaling-up concurrent OLAP workloads presents an opportunity of exploiting sharing across concurrent queries. (b) Scaling-up a NUMA-agnostic aggregation hits a bottleneck before completely saturating CPU resources.

queries cannot be serviced in parallel and independently, the effect of sharing across queries becomes apparent in the total response time. Sharing scans can decrease the response time considerably by sharing the scans of common relations of all queries at the I/O layer. Further sharing of higher operators in the query plans can further decrease response time [119, 120].

The second challenge is the non-uniform memory access (NUMA) architecture of modern multisocket multicore servers [87]. In the previous chapter, we show that the non-uniformity of the latency of memory accesses plays a significant role in scaling-up OLTP workloads. OLAP workloads are equally concerned with an additional non-uniform resource: the memory bandwidth. Figure 5.1b visualizes this challenge. It shows the throughput of an experiment that involves a single client issuing an aggregation query. In a typical execution engine, increasing the number of threads with which the aggregation is parallelized, up to the number of available hardware contexts of the machine, results in an analogous increase of the throughput that plateaus shortly before the number of available hardware contexts. On modern multisocket multicore machines, however, that may not be the case. For a typical NUMA-agnostic execution engine that relies on the operating system for its data placement and thread scheduling across the machine's sockets, it is probable that the throughput will hit a plateau much earlier than the number of available hardware contexts. The reason in this example is that the data to be aggregated happens to be allocated on a single socket, and the throughput is limited by the maximum bandwidth supported by that socket [121]. A NUMA-aware execution engine that explicitly handles its data placement and thread scheduling across the machine's sockets can fully utilize the memory bandwidth of both sockets and significantly increase the achieved throughput in this example [121].

In this chapter, we explore the two aforementioned challenges and explain how to exploit sharing opportunities that arise in highly concurrent analytical workloads, and also how to avoid NUMA-related problems. In Section 5.1, we survey the sharing methodologies available in related work, and focus on two state-of-the-art techniques. In Section 5.2, we detail several NUMA-aware solutions in related work. We begin with black-box approaches, then present DBMS-specific data placement and task scheduling solutions.

5.1   SHARING ACROSS CONCURRENT QUERIES

A typical relational data warehouse accepts a few analytical queries and consumes I/O, RAM, and CPU resources to evaluate each query separately, following a query-centric model [47]. The era of big data introduces new challenges to analytical processing [62, 63]. Among them, the data warehouse is called upon to handle an ever-increasing number of bigger, more complex, longer-running queries. Naturally, the traditional query-centric model that evaluates each query independently results in contention for resources. For performance this means delays in processing the queries, or an admission control policy that may delay new queries until resources are freed.

Sharing is one technique that can alleviate the contention for resources. In the case that queries share similar parts, we can reuse parts of data and the execution to save resources. By *sharing data*, we refer to coordinating I/O requests, sharing data among queries, and avoiding unnecessary data copying and referencing, while by *sharing work*, we refer to saving CPU resources, by avoiding redundant computations [118]. By saving resources, we reduce contention for resources. With more free resources, we can evaluate more concurrent queries and this translates to better performance such as increased throughput.

Even in typical query-centric databases, where queries are optimized and executed independently without sharing among concurrent queries, there are sharing techniques: caching [140], materialized views [135], multi-query optimization with the exploitation of common subexpressions [45, 138], and buffer pool management techniques [136]. More contemporary, state-of-the-art sharing techniques, however, share across concurrent queries at run-time, after query optimization. *Reactive sharing* shares common intermediate results of common subplans among queries [47, 120]. *Proactive sharing* takes a different approach to developing shared operators that can evaluate a high number of similar queries, composing a global query plan with shared operators for all the query mix [12, 22, 48, 120]. Both reactive and proactive sharing use shared scans, such as the one of Section 2.3. Next, we give more details on reactive and proactive sharing.

5.1.1   REACTIVE SHARING

Let us assume two queries that share a common sub-plan below an operator, e.g., a join operator, but have two different operators on top of them, e.g., aggregation operators, as shown in Figure 5.2a [118]. The query-centric model, with pipelining, evaluates them separately using intermediate FIFO buffers to exchange pages of tuples.

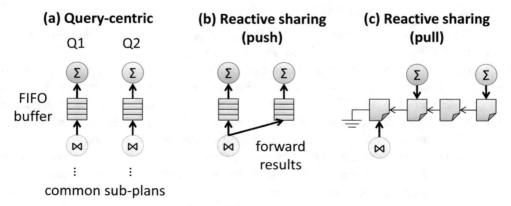

Figure 5.2: (a) Evaluating two common sub-plans with a query-centric execution engine. (b) Reactive sharing through pushing common intermediate results. (c) Reactive sharing through pulling common intermediate results.

Reactive sharing was introduced in the QPipe execution engine [56]. It detects the common sub-plans, evaluates only one of them, and copies common results to the FIFO buffers of the two different aggregation operators. The amount of common intermediate results that can be shared depends on the inter-arrival delay of the common sub-plans and the top operator of the sub-plans [56]. Reactive sharing is shown in Figure 5.2b. The original proposal for reactive sharing uses a "push-based" model, because the single producer is responsible for forwarding the common tuples.

Push-based reactive sharing, however, has a significant drawback: it creates a serialization point. Subsequent operators, e.g., the aggregations of the example, are delayed until incoming tuples are received. In certain cases of low concurrency, the serialization point makes the query-centric model better than reactive sharing since the queries move independently, exploiting available resources. Moreover, a prediction model has been proposed that can dynamically decide whether to use the query-centric model or reactive sharing [64].

Another approach to reactive sharing is pulling common intermediate results [119]. It shares common intermediate results without forwarding them. This eliminates the serialization point. The single producer independently emits pages of tuples at the head of a linked list, as shown in Figure 5.2c. Each consumer also walks the list independently from the tail up to the head, reading the common intermediate results. The serialization point is eliminated since the producer now independently emits tuples, at the speed of the query-centric model, without a need to forward tuples to multiple consumers. More importantly, there is no need for a prediction model to decide whether to use the query-centric model or reactive sharing. Thus, reactive sharing can be implemented with a low overhead for sharing common intermediate results at run-time.

5.1.2   PROACTIVE SHARING

The main drawback of reactive sharing is that it only shares common sub-plans, with common predicates for the involved operators. Reactive sharing cannot, for example, share the join operator of two queries if they have different selection predicates for the joined relations, as shown in Figure 5.3a. Proactive sharing, however, can share across these concurrent queries. Proactive sharing was introduced in the CJOIN operator [22]. Proactive sharing uses *shared operators* that can evaluate many similar queries concurrently, in a global query plan. The basic technique used to achieve this is attaching a bitmap to tuples, thereby showing the relevant queries from the query mix for which the tuples qualify. A shared operator indirectly exploits common instructions (see Section 3.5), as it evaluates the same instructions for multiple similar queries.

Lets go through the example of Figure 5.3a to see how a global query plan can be built with shared scans, selections, and hash-joins to evaluate these two queries [118]. Let us assume that the right-hand side (RHS) of the hash-join is the smaller relation for which we build the hash table. Tuples from the RHS relation flow into the shared selection operator, which outputs tuples with an attached bitmap that signify whether each tuple is relevant to one of the queries.

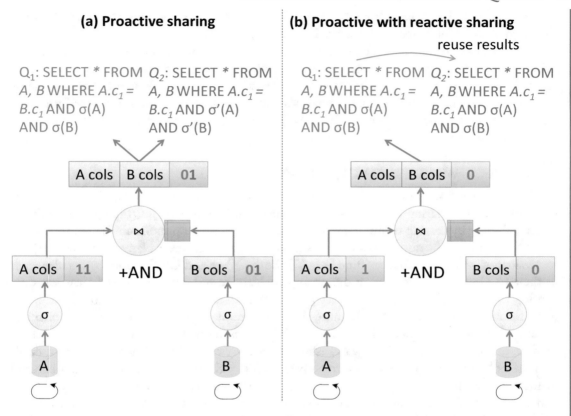

Figure 5.3: (a) Proactive sharing with two queries sharing a similar plan but different selection predicates for the joined relations. (b) Reactive sharing on top of proactive sharing.

After the hash table has been built, tuples from the left-hand side (LHS) relation flow in the same fashion to the join operator. The hash-join proceeds as usual and output joined tuples are produced. What it does in addition, however, is a bitwise AND operation between the bitmaps of the joined tuples in order to preserve the relevance of the output tuple to the queries. In this example, because the RHS tuple was not selected by Q_1, the output tuple is also not selected by Q_1. Additional similar queries joining the same relations, with the same join predicate, but different selection predicates can be added dynamically and evaluated by this single shared hash-join, simply by extending the bitmaps.

In contrast to the query-centric model, proactive sharing has an overhead, which is most apparent for a low number of concurrent queries. Proactive sharing needs an additional admission phase for a new incoming query to adjust the global query plan to accommodate the new query [12, 22, 119]. Also, there is additional bookkeeping overhead as shown, e.g., by the additional bitmaps and bitmap computations [119]. Nevertheless, the benefits of proactive sharing for a high number of concurrent queries dwarf the overhead [48, 119].

Proactive sharing and reactive sharing are orthogonal. For example, if the two exemplary queries are identical, they still pass through the global query plan; even if they produce the same intermediate results, their bitmaps are the same and we do redundant work. In such a case, we can combine both sharing techniques and apply reactive sharing on top of proactive sharing [119], as shown in Figure 5.3b. Reactive sharing reuses the results of Q_1 and avoids redundant computations and bitwise operations for Q_2.

5.1.3   SYSTEMS WITH SHARING TECHNIQUES

In Table 5.1, we show the systems and research prototypes that introduced and advanced reactive and proactive sharing techniques across concurrent queries [119]. QPipe [56] introduced reactive sharing by sharing common intermediate results across common sub-plans at run-time. CJOIN introduced the notion of proactive sharing with a global query plan of shared hash-joins for evaluating star queries at run-time [22, 23]. Both QPipe and CJOIN employ circular scans in their I/O layer. CJOIN uses an online approach for re-ordering the shared hash-joins according to the selectivities of the queries [22]. DataPath advanced the notion of global query plans for more general schemas and more shared operators [12]. It also supports an optimizer for adapting the global query plan due to a newly incoming query. At its I/O layer, DataPath employs a linear scan of a disk array to sustain a very large throughput. SharedDB [48] specialized the notion of global query plans for mixed OLTP and OLAP workload by using batched in-memory execution, a precomputed global query plan, and circular scans that process read and update requests. Batched execution has also been shown to avoid unnecessary overhead in hash-joins by sharing the build phase and efficiently updating hash tables for new queries [95]. A heuristic algorithm has been proposed in the context of SharedDB to generate the global query plan by considering the whole query mix [49].

Table 5.1: Systems that employ sharing techniques across concurrent queries.

System	QPipe [56]	CJOIN [22, 23]	DataPath [12]	SharedDB [48, 49]
Sharing technique	Reactive	Proactive (Global Query Plan)		
Execution	Dynamic	Dynamic	Dynamic	Batched
Schema	General	Star	General	General (precomputed)
I/O	Circular scans	Circular scans	Linear scan of a disk array	Main-memory circular scans

Most systems using sharing focus on OLAP workloads, as analytical read-mostly workloads are amenable to sharing [118]. Sharing, however, can be useful for OLTP workloads as well. Reactive and proactive sharing techniques can be used across the same version of data under a multi-version concurrency control [22, 23]. SharedDB effectively supports proactive sharing in mixed OLTP and OLAP workloads by operating on versioned data through the combination of batched execution and the usage of circular scans that process read and update requests [48].

In conclusion, a big data analytical system should employ sharing across concurrent queries to share data and work. For cases of low concurrency, the system can use query-centric operators, along with reactive sharing at run-time. For highly concurrent workloads, the system can employ proactive sharing to build a global query plan to evaluate the whole query mix, and can additionally employ reactive sharing whenever there is a sharing opportunity for common sub-plans [119].

5.2   NUMA-AWARENESS

The significance of NUMA-aware data placement and scheduling in order to optimize for faster local memory accesses has been prominent since a long time ago in the systems community. When NUMA architectures emerged, related work studied the advantages and disadvantages of cache-coherent (ccNUMA) and cache-only memory architectures (COMA) designs which can dynamically cache remote memory pages [39, 144]. Currently, ccNUMA designs prevail for modern multisocket multicore servers [28].

Figure 5.4 shows a modern ccNUMA server, with four sockets, each having a 15-core Intel Xeon E7-4880 v2 2.50 GHz (Ivybridge-EX) processor [123]. The depicted configuration has four 16 GB DIMM per memory controller (MC). The sockets are interconnected to enable accessing remote memory of another socket. Each socket has 3 Intel QPI (QuickPath Interconnect) links. Each QPI has a 16 GB/s bandwidth that supports data requests and the cache coherence protocol.

NUMA allows hardware vendors to support multiple sockets with a large number of hardware contexts on a machine. Compared to traditional machine architectures with uniform memory accesses, however, they introduce new considerations for software performance [17, 118, 123]. These are enumerated in Figure 5.4 and outlined here:

1. The memory bandwidth of a single socket can be separately saturated.

2. The memory bandwidth of an interconnect can be separately saturated.

3. Accesses to remote memory are slower than accesses to local memory.

Especially for the second point, it is important to note that interconnects can easily become a performance bottleneck due to their limited memory bandwidth [28, 118]. Although the bandwidth of interconnects may be improved with every new processor generation, it is typically lower than the memory bandwidth of a single socket. Additionally, an interconnect can become a bottleneck in large NUMA topologies when it needs to route remote traffic to multiple sockets.

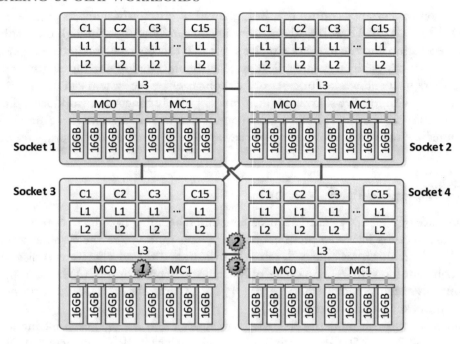

Figure 5.4: A server with four sockets of 15-core Intel Xeon E7-4880 v2 2.50 GHz (Ivybridge-EX) processors. NUMA introduces additional performance bottlenecks points (enumerated in the figure) that the software needs to consider.

The software needs to tackle the aforementioned issues by becoming NUMA-aware. NUMA-awareness is achieved by optimizing for local memory accesses instead of remote accesses, and avoiding unnecessary centralized bandwidth bottlenecks of either sockets or interconnects [118]. Black-box NUMA-aware approaches have been proposed that track and predict the memory accesses of the applications, either by instrumenting applications or by using hardware counters, in order to migrate and/or replicate memory pages [21, 88, 105]. For example, the DINO scheduler monitors the cache behavior of applications' threads and tries to move them and their data to balance cache load and improve cache efficiency [18]. As another example, Carrefour re-organizes data with replication, interleaving, or co-location in order to avoid memory bottlenecks [34]. Nevertheless, the main disadvantage of black box approaches is that they do not use application knowledge and may not always be optimal for DBMS [18, 164], because DBMS can be unpredictable as they handle various workloads and can change behavior at run-time.

For this reason, we need to use application knowledge inside the execution engine to efficiently support NUMA-awareness. NUMA-awareness can improve the performance of by several factors [77, 123]. A prominent example of a static black-box approach tailored for DBMS is presented by Giceva et al. [50] to characterize and group the shared operators of a predefined global query plan, and place them on a NUMA server with the main aim of improving overall energy efficiency. Figure 5.5 shows the main deployment algorithm of this black-box approach. The algorithm collapses operators together by examining the global query plan, and then special Resource Activity Vectors (RAV) are calculated for the operators by calibrating them and measuring their core performance characteristics before the actual deployment of the global query plan onto the cores of the NUMA server. The RAV contain information about the performance characteristics and requirements of the shared operator, such as IPC, average memory bandwidth, etc. Finally, the actual deployment scheme is decided using information about the topology and the characteristics of the NUMA server. The experiments of the author show that the same performance can be achieved as a NUMA-agnostic deployment of the global query plan, but with 14% of utilized CPU resources.

5.2.1 ANALYTICAL OPERATORS

In this section, we present NUMA-aware analytical algorithms and operations specific to DBMS or NUMA-aware implementations of analytical operators.

We start with a general approach to data exchange: data shuffling. In data shuffling, there are N producers and N consumers across the sockets of a NUMA server. Each producer parti-

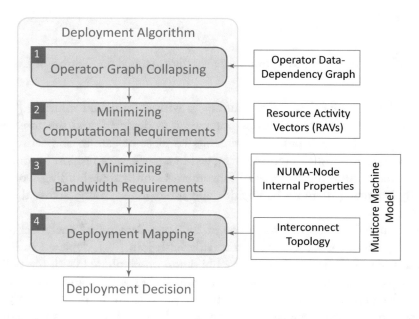

Figure 5.5: A DBMS-specific black-box approach for deploying a global query plan on a NUMA server. (Based on Figure 4 of Giceva et al. [50].)

tions its data into N pieces and wants to transmit its piece of data to all consumers. The naïve way of data shuffling is shown in Figure 5.6a. In the first step, all producers transmit their data to the first consumer, then to the second consumer, and so on. This naïve way actually creates a centralized memory bandwidth bottleneck since the consumer is on one socket while the producers are on multiple sockets, which results in bad performance [94].

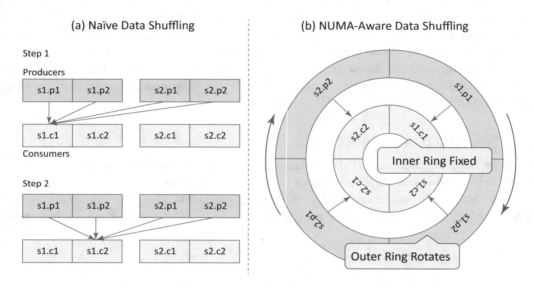

Figure 5.6: (a) Naïve vs. (b) NUMA-aware data shuffling. (Based on Figure 5 of Li et al. [94].)

A more clever way of doing data shuffling is with coordinated shuffling [94], shown in Figure 5.6b. The producers are put in the outer ring, as depicted, and the consumers are put in the inner ring, so that each producer transmits its piece of data to one consumer. In order to complete the algorithm, the outer ring is moved in a clock-wise fashion for one full circle so that the producers transmit their data to all consumers. Coordinated shuffling avoids centralized bottlenecks by balancing memory bandwidth and interconnect traffic across the sockets of a NUMA server.

We continue with joins which are one of the most demanding analytical operations. A very popular algorithm for hash-joins is the radix hash-join [78], depicted in Figure 5.7. In comparison to the typical hash-join with the build and probe phase [129], the radix hash-join first partitions each relation to partitions that fit into caches with a radix partitioning scheme, and then joins the partitions. After bringing the partitions from the memory to the caches, the join occurs only by accessing the caches, and this cache-efficiency makes the radix hash-join have a very good performance. More advantages include less collisions on the hash tables, and less TLB misses [78]. The problem for modern multisocket multicore servers, however, is that the radix hash-join is not NUMA-aware. It does not take into account where the relations are physically allocated, and the algorithm may access them remotely.

Albutiu et al. [9] developed a NUMA-aware join operator based on sort-merge join, called Massively Parallel Sort-Merge (MPSM) join. The MPSM is based on three rules for NUMA-awareness [9] and outlined here.

1. Remote random writes should be avoided.

2. Sequential random reads are allowed.

3. Synchronization should be avoided.

Figure 5.8 shows how MPSM works with two relations on a NUMA server with three sockets (visualized with different colors). The relations R and S are partitioned to partitions that are sorted locally on the sockets. Each partition of the outer relation is then merged with every partition of the inner relation. Because the inner partitions are scanned, the prefetcher can hide the increased latency cost of remote accesses. It has been shown that MPSM is faster than the radix hash-join on NUMA servers for star schemas [9], where the outer relation is a large fact table and the inner relation a significantly smaller dimension table [80].

A later study, however, shows that radix hash join is still the superior join algorithm [15]. MPSM suffers from bandwidth saturation for general schemas, as large remote partitions during the merge phase need to be scanned, which saturates interconnects and remote memory controllers. The authors of the study advance MPSM by making their own optimized version of sort-merge join using SIMD and multiway merging to avoid bandwidth saturation. By using

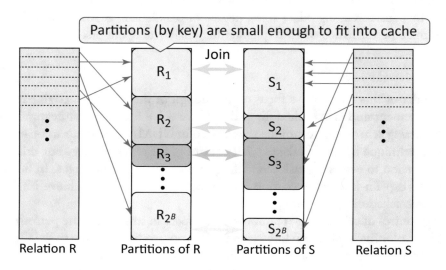

Figure 5.7: The radix hash-join. (Based on Figure 1 of Kim et al. [78].)

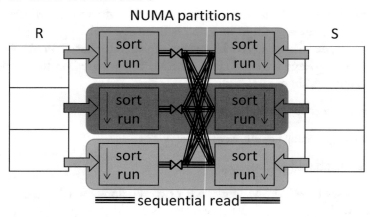

Figure 5.8: The massively parallel sort-merge join (MPSM) algorithm. (Based on Figure 2 of Albutiu et al. [9].)

task scheduling (see Section 5.2.2), they can balance CPU and memory bandwidth utilization to avoid centralized bottlenecks. Still, their radix hash-join implementation proves to be better. Figure 5.9 shows the results of the authors comparing the three different join algorithms for the same dataset, joining 2 tables with 16 billion tuples, using 64 threads, on the same NUMA server which is a 4-socket server with Intel Sandy Bridge processors.

The long-standing battle between different join algorithms in the recent literature shows that NUMA is just one factor for achieving efficient performance. There are many more factors that need to be considered, e.g., data sizes, degree of parallelism, SIMD instructions, etc., in order to optimize performance when implementing analytical operators.

5.2.2   TASK SCHEDULING

In the remainder of this chapter, we focus on the design of the execution engine for NUMA-aware data placement and CPU scheduling. Before we delve into the architectural details, we focus on a recurring scheduling technique that is used in NUMA-aware execution engines: task scheduling, a technique allows to take explicit control of CPU scheduling. For this reason, we dedicate this section to exploring task scheduling, its benefits and challenges. In Section 5.2.3, we continue to explain how an execution engine can be designed to achieve NUMA-aware coordinated task scheduling and data placement.

Taking control of scheduling is an important aspect in improving the performance of an application by exploiting application knowledge that is not readily available to the OS scheduler. Let us consider the case where we leave scheduling to the OS. In the most typical case, one thread is created per query. If the incoming queries are more than the hardware threads of the server, then the hardware threads are "oversubscribed." In order to accommodate the software threads,

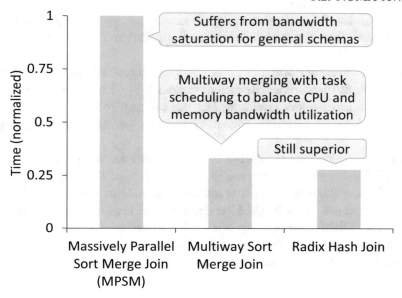

Figure 5.9: A comparison of NUMA-aware join algorithms. (Based on Figure 18 of Balkesen et al. [15].)

the OS arranges timeslots for the utilization of the hardware threads. Figure 5.10 shows an example of oversubscription and a schedule of timeslots arranged by the OS for accommodating three software threads with one hardware thread.

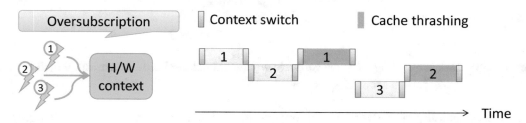

Figure 5.10: Timeslots arranged by the OS scheduler in the case of oversubscription of hardware threads. Context switches and possible cache thrashing are two negative side effects.

There are two main performance problems of oversubscription [122]. First, there are context switches between the timeslots, as the software thread that currently runs on the hardware thread is pre-empted in order to run another software thread. Second, there can be potential cache thrashing if an upcoming thread invalidates useful data brought to the cache by the previous thread. Furthermore, in heterogeneous co-processor environments, it has been shown that oversubscription can lead to performance degradation when multiple operators run in parallel on a co-processor and their accumulated memory footprint exceeds the main memory capacity of the co-processor [19].

To partly avoid these performance problems, DBMS typically use a query admission control mechanism to limit the number concurrent queries [58]. A query admission control, however, takes action on a per-query level and does not necessarily avoid an excessive number of concurrent threads during the whole workload execution, especially if intra-query parallelism is used [122].

A better or complementary solution is to use task scheduling, which has been widely adopted in DBMS and research prototypes [3, 19, 20, 83, 91, 122, 124]. This is shown in Figure 5.11. DBMS encapsulate all of their workload into units of work called "tasks" which are enqueued into task queues. On a NUMA server, there can be, for example, one task queue per socket [83, 91, 124]. DBMS then employ one worker thread per hardware thread. Each worker thread continuously queries the task queues for tasks to execute. Since there are no more software threads presented to the OS, oversubscription performance problems are avoided.

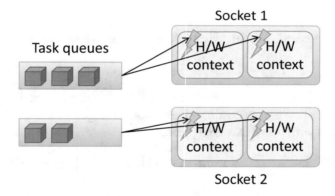

Figure 5.11: Task scheduling uses one software worker thread per hardware thread, which continuously process tasks from a set of task queues.

Task scheduling provides numerous opportunities, but also presents several challenges [35, 122, 159, 167]. Among the opportunities are the following. First, task scheduling allows to decouple the application's scheduling from the OS scheduler. The advantage is that the application can take full control and predictability of its scheduling. Second, it can control task granularity and scheduling to balance between CPU-intensive and memory-demanding tasks [15]. Third, task prioritization can support workload management techniques [125].

Some of the main challenges of task scheduling are the following. First, task queues may have an unbalanced number and duration of tasks. One solution is to use a form of task stealing in order to load balance worker threads: when a task queue is empty, the worker thread can search other task queues to steal tasks from. An alternative solution for scheduling parallel loops is to distribute batches of loop iterations via shared counters, a method which dispenses with work queues [57]. Second, tasks may block or sleep in due to synchronization. The OS may leave a hardware thread unused if it does not have knowledge of other worker threads that it can schedule while a task blocks. The solution is to detect when a worker thread may become inactive and schedule another active worker thread in order to avoid underutilization [122]. Third, task granularity can become a challenge for task scheduling. Task granularity can be correlated with the level of saturation of the machine in order to avoid too fine-grained tasks that can present significant scheduling overhead, but also avoid too coarse-grained tasks that can decrease parallelism [122].

5.2.3   COORDINATED DATA PLACEMENT AND TASK SCHEDULING

In this section, we continue with describing the design of NUMA-aware execution engines. NUMA-awareness spans two dimensions that need to be coordinated: (a) scheduling tasks onto sockets and (b) placing data across sockets. The design of the task scheduler should allow for a task to have an affinity for a socket. The task scheduler, for example, can employ a pool of worker threads and a task queue per socket. Inter-socket task stealing may be employed. With respect to data placement, DBMS need to know where its data structures are placed and take their location into account when scheduling tasks onto sockets. By coordinating scheduling and data placement, DBMS can prefer local memory accesses, avoid unnecessary bandwidth bottlenecks, and become NUMA-aware [118].

With respect to data placement, NUMA-aware DBMS fall into two broad categories: (a) static solutions and (b) adaptive solutions. Static solutions do not attempt to modify data placement in order to optimize the performance of the running workload. They are suitable for workloads that are known in advance, but cannot necessarily handle efficiently ad-hoc workloads. Adaptive solutions are best suited for ad-hoc workloads that the system needs to execute in a NUMA-aware fashion, but may incur an overhead in analyzing the workload at hand and may need fine-tuning to adapt to fast-changing workloads [118].

A lot of DBMS that do not mention advanced NUMA optimizations, and indirectly rely on the first-touch policy for data placement, fall in this category [118]. A further example is HyPer [91], which chunks and distributes "morsels" of data across the sockets. The basic architecture of HyPer is shown in Figure 5.12, with an example of a server with two sockets (red and blue) and a query that joins tables R, S, and T with hash-joins. For the query execution, HyPer first creates the hash tables for tables S and T. Then each worker thread takes a morsel from the bigger relation R from its respective socket and passes it through the hash tables to evaluate the join and outputs the joined tuples to a NUMA-aware local result buffer. The "Dispatcher" component is actually HyPer's task scheduler, with task stealing enabled.

In the realm of adaptive solutions for data placement, ERIS [83] is a NUMA-aware storage manager that efficiently supports shared scans and shared index lookups. The design of ERIS is shown in Figure 5.13. ERIS uses task scheduling so that each worker thread, called

Autonomous Execution Unit (AEU), is assigned a specific partition of a data object to service. The real power of ERIS comes from its dynamic load balancing. It dynamically detects changes to the workload, and rebalances the partitions across worker threads in order to improve the performance of the overall workload on the NUMA server.

In contrast to HyPer and ERIS, which both heavily partition data across sockets, a research prototype on top of SAP HANA [124] proposes to avoid unnecessary partitioning due to overhead in query processing. An adaptive data placement strategy is proposed that first prefers to move data across sockets, and partitions data only when necessary in order to balance active data and local accesses across sockets. An example is shown in Figure 5.14. The authors further propose that inter-socket task stealing should also be adaptive: tasks with a high memory throughput should not be stolen across sockets, or else there is overhead due to saturated interconnects and sockets.

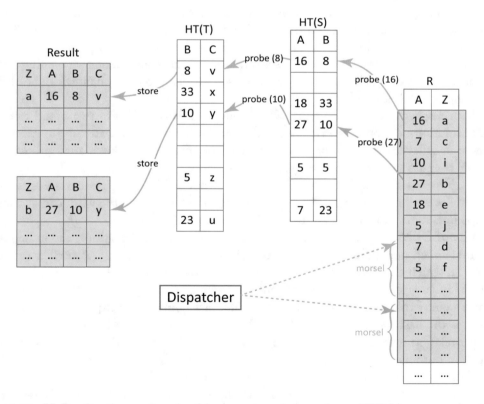

Figure 5.12: HyPer distributes morsels of data across sockets, and uses NUMA-aware task scheduling. (Based on Figure 1 of Leis et al. [91].)

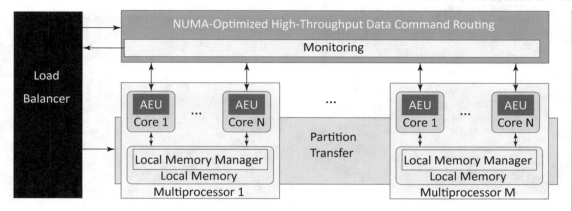

Figure 5.13: The design of ERIS. (Based on Figure 3 of Kissinger et al. [83].)

5.3   CONCLUSIONS

To summarize this chapter, there are two basic dimensions that DBMS need to consider when scaling-up OLAP workloads on modern multicore servers. First, DBMS need to exploit sharing opportunities across concurrent queries, by employing reactive and proactive sharing techniques, in order to avoid redundant work, reduce contention for resources, and improve overall performance. Second, DBMS need to be NUMA-aware and consider the non-uniformity of the underlying multisocket multicore server. DBMS need coordinated data placement and task

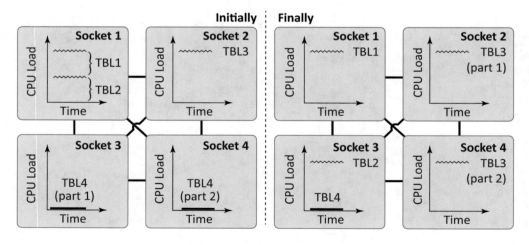

Figure 5.14: Adaptive data placement by first moving data and then partitioning data [124].

scheduling in order to favor local memory accesses over remote memory accesses and avoid unnecessary memory bandwidth bottlenecks.

PART III

Conclusions

CHAPTER 6

Outlook

In this chapter, we outline a few of the most prominent future directions of databases on modern and novel hardware. These future directions may require a substantial redesign of database systems in order to fully exploit the potential of novel hardware and answer the challenges posed by emerging workloads.

One of the major opportunities for improving efficiency of data management systems is utilizing specialized hardware inspired by the rise of dark silicon (see Section 6.1). Namely, increasing power requirements of modern multicores make keeping all cores powered on difficult and many researchers propose different types of accelerators that can be used instead of general purpose cores.

Another trend includes changes in traditional memory and storage hierarchy and improved processor capabilities that have potential to radically simplify the design of data management systems. Non-volatile RAM, whose potential we discuss in Section 6.2, offers persistence almost at the latency of main memory thus eliminating major source of latency in the critical path of OLTP applications that require durability and alleviating the need to find other processing to overlap the latency of making data durable. Similarly, hardware transactional memory (surveyed briefly in Section 6.3) reduces the complexity of thread synchronization, especially for short critical sections.

Finally, increasingly complex applications built on top of data management platforms require both efficient processing of mixed OLTP and OLAP workloads and improving the energy efficiency of the database system (see Section 6.4).

6.1 DARK SILICON AND HARDWARE SPECIALIZATION

Looking ahead, a significant challenge is the rise of dark silicon [52, 53]. Even if twice the transistors fit in a unit of area according to Moore's law, the voltage required to power them does not decrease proportionally. This trend is depicted in Figure 6.1. In the near future, parts of the silicon will not be able to be powered. The unusable area of the chip is called "dark silicon," depicted with a black color in Figure 6.1.

The main idea of how dark silicon can be exploited is hardware specialization. Figure 6.1 depicts an example of specialized cores on the chip, visualized with different colors. The specialized cores can be dynamically cherry-picked based on the task at hand while the rest of the silicon remains dark and not powered.

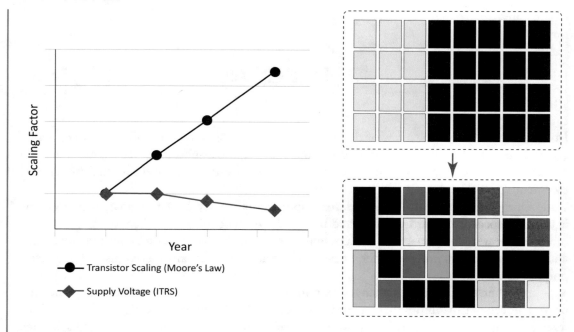

Figure 6.1: Trends of transistor scaling and supply voltage, based on Hardavellas et al. [52, 53] (left). How to exploit dark silicon with hardware specialization (right).

This direction has already been explored in a variety of different ways. Kocberber et al. [85] propose specialized cores for accelerated hash-joins, focusing on the hash index lookups. Wu et al. [166] design a collection of heterogeneous ASICs, with an instruction set, focusing on analytical operations. Their experimental results, however, show decreasing benefits with higher data sizes. Mueller et al. [100] propose the use of FPGAs for data analytics and streaming. Johnson et al. [65] set a vision of putting some database operations on FPGAs for transactions. Finally, Putnam et al. [126] propose reconfigurable data centers using FPGAs, and showcase how Bing's search can be accelerated.

One of the more unexplored questions around hardware specialization is how to easily and efficiently utilize the novel hardware? The whole software stack, including the OS and the applications, needs to be adapted in order to exploit hardware specialization. Compilers can be helpful in generating specialized code dynamically for heterogeneous hardware environments [73, 84].

6.2   NON-VOLATILE RAM AND DURABILITY

I/O is one of the main factors that limits throughput of OLTP systems regardless of their multi-core scalability. In well-tuned systems with sufficiently large main memory, the only I/O in the critical path occurs when writing logs. The emergence of non-volatile RAM (NVRAM) [110] has inspired many researchers to reconsider the techniques for achieving durability, mainly through work in two directions: (a) by optimizing the algorithms for write-ahead logging (WAL) and (b) by doing away with WAL and instead designing durable data structures.

One approach for taking advantage of NVRAM is by re-architecting group commit protocol to use NVRAM as a staging buffer for a batch of transactions [110]. This technique offers attractive improvements even with small amounts of NVRAM. A more elaborate passive group commit approach takes this idea further by making log buffers durable, using global sequence numbers and a distributed log design [162]. Finally, non-volatile logging techniques aim to minimize the overhead of logging for each individual transaction [61].

On the side of durable data structures, proposals include a write atomic cache-aware B-tree design [27] and a family of in-memory recoverable data structures [31]. While these data structures show good promise, using their full potential requires rethinking other components of the system. One such approach is suggested in conjunction with the write behind logging protocol proposal [11].

6.3   HARDWARE TRANSACTIONAL MEMORY

Transactional memory was introduced by Herlihy and Moss over 20 years ago [60]. In their seminal paper, they argue that lock-free data structures avoid common problems locking techniques exhibit, such as priority inversion, convoying, and deadlocks, and that transactional memory makes lock-free synchronization as efficient as the lock-based one. They define a transaction as a sequence of instructions that is atomic and serializable, and argue that it can be implemented as a straightforward extension of the cache coherence protocol. Interestingly, two early commercial implementations use completely different implementations of hardware transactional memory compared to the original proposal. Sun's prototype Rock processor relies on speculative execution to implement best-effort HTM [37], while IBM's BlueGene/Q processor uses multiversioned last-level cache with unmodified cores and L1 caches for the same purpose [161].

Intel Transactional Synchronization Extension (TSX) is the new instruction set that appears in Intel's Haswell line of processors and enables transactional memory support in hardware. It is closer in spirit to the original HTM proposal than the previous commercial implementations. TSX instructions are implemented as an extension of the cache-coherency protocol, so they keep track of what memory addresses are accessed at a cache-line granularity. Current implementation is limited to the L1 data caches that are used to store both read and write sets of a transaction. The associativity of the cache (8 in current processors) as well as the size of the cache limits the size of these sets. An eviction of a write address from the cache always causes an abort. At the same time, a read address may be evicted from the cache before a transaction ends without causing an abort, due to limited support in cache coherence protocols for the private L2 caches.

TSX instructions can be used in two ways, through Hardware Lock Elision (HLE) and Restricted Transactional Memory (RTM) modes. Hardware Lock Elision is a legacy compatible

API inspired by speculative lock elision (SLE) technique that improves performance of lock-based programs when critical sections could have been executed without locks [128]. Restricted transactional memory provides Haswell specific instructions XBEGIN, XEND, and XABORT that allows explicit control over hardware transactions.

Hardware transactional memory (HTM) is a very promising approach to efficient synchronization that has inspired a lot of recent research following Intel's implementation in the Haswell line of processors. Nevertheless, it is not a silver bullet, especially for scalability challenges in mature software systems.

For example, recent research has shown that HTM is attractive for low contention scenarios and can be combined with spinlocks to implement an efficient lock manager in a database system [157]. It can also improve performance of operations on common tree index structures [72], however using it for acceleration of many types of critical sections in a mature system exposes severe limitations with respect to duration and size of critical sections and can even decrease the performance of the system [25]. Hence, efficiently utilizing HTM requires a fundamental redesign of the OLTP system components.

The HyPer team has proposed a very low overhead concurrency control mechanism that combines timestamp ordering with short hardware transactions [92]. Finally, a recent proposal demonstrates that a design tuned for Intel's HTM implementation can offer performance comparable to a state-of-the-art main memory transaction processing system with fine-grained locks while having lower code complexity [163].

6.4 TASK SCHEDULING FOR MIXED WORKLOADS AND ENERGY EFFICIENCY

From the software side, two novel requirements that database designers are called to satisfy are the efficient processing of mixed OLTP and OLAP workloads, and improving the overall energy efficiency of the database. For both of these requirements, related work shows that task scheduling (see Chapter 5) can be a useful and helpful technique in satisfying them.

With respect to mixed workloads, DBMS were, until recently, categorized into OLTP-oriented solutions, which process transactions on fresh operational data, and OLAP-oriented solutions which work on a replicated outdated version of the operational data to process heavyweight analytical workloads. Nowadays, this separation is not suited for realtime reporting. Organizations increasingly need analytics on fresh operational data to gain a competitive advantage or obtain insight about fast-breaking situations [5, 106, 125]. Examples [125] can include online games that make special offers based on non-trivial analysis [24], liquidity and risk analysis, which benefit from fresh data while also requiring complex analytical queries [112], and fraud detection analyzing continuously arriving transactional data [104]. For this reason, real-time reporting has resulted in the development of DBMS that efficiently support mixed OLTP and OLAP workloads on a common schema [112]. Examples include main-memory DBMS such as SAP HANA [40] and HyPer [76]. It has been shown that there are three major factors affecting the performance of mixed workloads while the number of concurrent clients is scaled [125]: (a) data freshness; (b) transactional and analytical query flexibility; and (c) scheduling. Scheduling has been shown to be of major significance for the performance of mixed workloads. Typically, DBMS handling mixed workloads, such as SAP HANA [40] and HyPer [76], suffer from the "house effect", whereby an increasing number of heavyweight analytical queries overshadows the performance of concurrent lightweight transactions [125]. Task scheduling combined with workload management features, such as task prioritization, has been proposed as a potential solution to toggle the performance of mixed workload toward OLTP or OLAP as needed [125]. Another solution that has been recently proposed to support a high isolation of OLTP and OLAP performance is the logical separation of analytical queries and transactional updates using a single snapshot replica along with batch scheduling of queries and updates [96].

With respect to energy efficiency, dynamic task scheduling has been proposed to improve the overall energy efficiency of the workload, which encapsulates both performance and energy consumption, by dynamically toggling hardware features [121]. Such features include the dynamic voltage and frequency scaling (DVFS) features for each processor, which can regulate the operation frequency and thus energy consumption of processors, Turbo Boost, which can be applied on a few cores to overclock them when possible, and the different C-states or sleep modes, that provide different energy savings and speeds of sleeping and waking up [121]. A calibration phase is proposed to measure the performance and energy characteristics of operators under different parameters, such as number of threads, scheduling strategies and data placements. By using the resulting calibration curves, and measuring hardware counters at run-time, DBMS can make decisions on the task scheduling and data placement for the query mix and their respective operations in order to improve the general energy efficiency of the workload.

CHAPTER 7

Summary

Ever-increasing amounts of data captured with rapid rise in a variety of applications analyzing that data fuel the steady development of data management systems. Modern hardware offers increasing core counts, faster memories, and network interfaces, however, the changes in hardware architectures prevent software systems from automatically benefiting from hardware innovation. In this book, we set out to survey the challenges posed by modern multicore processors to data management software that prevent it from fully exploiting available processing power, both in the vertical dimension (core features and cache hierarchy) and the horizontal dimension (hardware parallelism and memory bandwidth).

In this book, we review several pieces of the literature that relate to the aforementioned dimensions. The most essential concepts are summarized in Figure 7.1. The figure contains the concepts of the hardware on the upper level, and the correlated software concepts on the bottom level that bridge the gap between hardware and software.

Our key takeaway is that in order to bridge the gap between software and hardware, DBMS needs to consider efficiency along the following three axes: exploiting hardware, work scheduling, and achieving scalability.

Exploiting hardware. Extracting the best performance from the modern hardware requires considering multiple facets of hardware in a holistic fashion. First, one should use all microarchitectural features, such as instruction level parallelism, SIMD, and multithreading, of each core that is powered on. Ideally, all of these cores should be used in order to amortize the idle power. Finally, one should efficiently access cache and memory hierarchy both on single socket and multisocket systems. It is important to keep in mind that most of the underutilization of cores comes from the fact that they stall because they are not provided as efficiently as possible the necessary instructions and data.

Work scheduling. Scheduling is a significant factor affecting the performance of database workloads. DBMS need to look at operations at the right task granularity while scheduling them in order to be able to make optimal decisions about memory management and resource utilization. Moreover, instructions and data require locality at different levels in the memory hierarchy; instructions need L1-I whereas data needs local RAM or LLC. Finally, it is important to ensure that memory bandwidth between processor and RAM as well as between processors is not saturated unnecessarily.

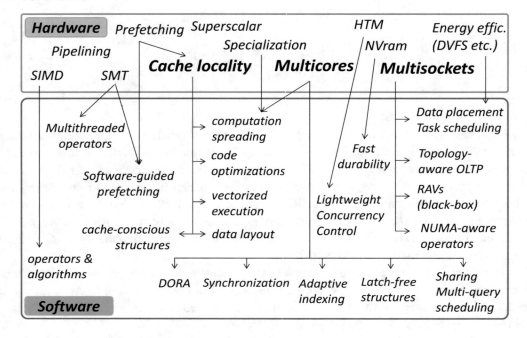

Figure 7.1: Summary of the hardware and software concepts we reviewed.

Achieving scalability. If DBMS are scaling-up efficiently on the current generation of hardware, this does not necessarily guarantee that they will scale-up efficiently on the next generation of hardware. Current performance characteristics do not forecast future performance behavior as data sizes and processing capabilities scale. Data management systems need to ensure that all their critical sections and communication points in the code avoid unbounded communication and maximize locality whenever possible.

Recently, there has been a flurry of interesting research results aimed at designing data management systems that fully exploit capabilities of modern hardware. Modern multicores processors have opened many research directions, a selection of which we highlight in this book. However, recent advances in storage and memory systems, as well as heterogeneous computing architectures, partly inspired by dark silicon, in addition to increasingly varied data management operations offer many more research opportunities.

Bibliography

[1] Intel Utilizing Software Prefetching.
https://software.intel.com/en-us/node/540518

[2] Intel Profile-Guided Optimizations Overview.
https://software.intel.com/en-us/node/522721

[3] Intel Thread Building Blocks—Documentation—User Guide—The Task Scheduler—Task-based Programming, June 2016.
http://threadingbuildingblocks.org/documentation

[4] MemSQL Documentation v5.8 – Code Generation.
https://docs.memsql.com/v5.8/docs/code-generation

[5] SAP HANA Live for SAP Business Suite, April 2016. http://help.sap.com/hba

[6] The Java HotSpot Performance Engine Architecture.
http://www.oracle.com/technetwork/java/whitepaper-135217.html

[7] Y. Ahmad, O. Kennedy, C. Koch, and M. Nikolic DBToaster: Higher-order Delta Processing for Dynamic, Frequently Fresh Views. *PVLDB*, 5(10):968–979, 2012. DOI: 10.14778/2336664.2336670.

[8] A. Ailamaki, D. J. DeWitt, M. D. Hill, and D. A. Wood. DBMSs on a modern processor: Where does time go? In *VLDB*, pages 266–277, 1999.

[9] M.-C. Albutiu, A. Kemper, and T. Neumann. Massively parallel sort-merge joins in main memory multi-core database systems. *PVLDB*, 5(10):1064–1075, 2012. DOI: 10.14778/2336664.2336678.

[10] M. Annavaram, J. M. Patel, and E. S. Davidson. Call graph prefetching for database applications. *ACM TOCS*, 21(4):412–444, 2003. DOI: 10.1145/945506.945509.

[11] J. Arulraj, M. Perron, and A. Pavlo. Write-behind logging. *PVLDB*, 10(4):337–348, 2016. DOI: 10.14778/3025111.3025116.

[12] S. Arumugam, A. Dobra, C. M. Jermaine, N. Pansare, and L. Perez. The DataPath system: A data-centric analytic processing engine for large data warehouses. In *SIGMOD*, pages 519–530, 2010. DOI: 10.1145/1807167.1807224.

[13] I. Atta, P. Tözün, A. Ailamaki, and A. Moshovos. SLICC: Self-assembly of instruction cache collectives for OLTP workloads. In *MICRO*, pages 188–198, 2012. DOI: 10.1109/micro.2012.26.

[14] I. Atta, P. Tözün, X. Tong, A. Ailamaki, and A. Moshovos. STREX: Boosting instruction cache reuse in OLTP workloads through stratified transaction execution. In *ISCA*, pages 273–284, 2013. DOI: 10.1145/2508148.2485946.

[15] C. Balkesen, G. Alonso, J. Teubner, and M. T. Ozsu. Multi-core, main-memory joins: Sort vs. hash revisited. *PVLDB*, 7(1), pages 85–96, 2014. DOI: 10.14778/2732219.2732227.

[16] L. A. Barroso, K. Gharachorloo, and E. Bugnion. Memory system characterization of commercial workloads. In *ISCA*, pages 3–14, 1998. DOI: 10.1109/isca.1998.694758.

[17] S. Blagodurov, S. Zhuravlev, M. Dashti, and A. Fedorova. A case for NUMA-aware contention management on multicore systems. In *USENIX ATC*, page 1, 2011. DOI: 10.1145/1854273.1854350.

[18] S. Blagodurov, S. Zhuravlev, A. Fedorova, and A. Kamali. A case for NUMA-aware contention management on multicore systems. In *PACT*, pages 557–558, 2010. DOI: 10.1145/1854273.1854350.

[19] S. Breß, H. Funke, A. Fedorova, and J. Teubner. Robust Query Processing in Co-Processor-accelerated Databases. In *SIGMOD*, pages 1891–1906, 2016. DOI: 10.1145/2882903.2882936.

[20] R. D. Blumofe, C. F. Joerg, B. C. Kuszmaul, C. E. Leiserson, K. H. Randall, and Y. Zhou. Cilk: An efficient multithreaded runtime system. In *PPoPP*, pages 207–216, 1995. DOI: 10.1145/209936.209958.

[21] W. J. Bolosky, M. L. Scott, R. P. Fitzgerald, R. J. Fowler, and A. L. Cox. NUMA policies and their relation to memory architecture. In *ASPLOS*, pages 212–221, 1991. DOI: 10.1145/106972.106994.

[22] G. Candea, N. Polyzotis, and R. Vingralek. A scalable, predictable join operator for highly concurrent data warehouses. *PVLDB*, 2(1):277–288, 2009. DOI: 10.14778/1687627.1687659.

[23] G. Candea, N. Polyzotis, and R. Vingralek. Predictable performance and high query concurrency for data analytics. *The VLDB Journal*, 20(2):227–248, April 2011. DOI: 10.1007/s00778-011-0221-2.

[24] T. Cao, M. Vaz Salles, B. Sowell, Y. Yue, A. Demers, J. Gehrke, and W. White. Fast checkpoint recovery algorithms for frequently consistent applications. In *SIGMOD*, pages 265–276, 2011. DOI: 10.1145/1989323.1989352.

[25] D. Cervini, D. Porobic, P. Tözün, and A. Ailamaki. Applying HTM to an OLTP system: No free lunch. In *DaMon*, page 7, 2015. DOI: 10.1145/2771937.2771946.

[26] K. Chakraborty, P. M. Wells, and G. S. Sohi. Computation spreading: Employing hardware migration to specialize CMP cores on-the-fly. In *ASPLOS*, pages 283–292, 2006. DOI: 10.1145/1168857.1168893.

[27] A. Chatzistergiou, M. Cintra, and S. D. Viglas. Rewind: Recovery write-ahead system for in-memory non-volatile data-structures. *PVLDB*, 8(5):497–508, 2015. DOI: 10.14778/2735479.2735483.

[28] G. Chatzopoulos, R. Guerraoui, T. Harris, and V. Trigonakis. Abstracting multi-core topologies with MCTOP. In *EuroSys*, 2017. DOI: 10.1145/3064176.3064194.

[29] S. Chen, P. B. Gibbons, and T. C. Mowry. Improving Index Performance through Prefetching. In *SIGMOD*, pages 235–246, 2001. DOI: 10.1145/376284.375688.

[30] S. Chen, P. B. Gibbons, T. C. Mowry, and G. Valentin. Fractal prefetching b+-trees: Optimizing both cache and disk performance. In *SIGMOD*, pages 157–168, 2002. DOI: 10.1145/564691.564710.

[31] S. Chen and Q. Jin. Persistent b+-trees in non-volatile main memory. *PVLDB*, 8(7):786–797, 2015. DOI: 10.14778/2752939.2752947.

[32] J. Chhugani, A. D. Nguyen, V. W. Lee, W. Macy, M. Hagog, Y.-K. Chen, A. Baransi, S. Kumar, and P. Dubey. Efficient implementation of sorting on multi-core simd cpu architecture. *PVLDB*, 1(2):1313–1324, 2008. DOI: 10.14778/1454159.1454171.

[33] ClouidSuite: A Benchmark Suite for Cloud Services. http://cloudsuite.ch/

[34] M. Dashti, A. Fedorova, J. Funston, F. Gaud, R. Lachaize, B. Lepers, V. Quéma, and M. Roth. Traffic management: A holistic approach to memory placement on NUMA systems. In *ASPLOS*, pages 381–394, 2013. DOI: 10.1145/2499368.2451157.

[35] J. Dees and P. Sanders. Efficient many-core query execution in main memory column-stores. In *ICDE*, pages 350–361, 2013. DOI: 10.1109/icde.2013.6544838.

[36] C. Diaconu, C. Freedman, E. Ismert, P.-A. Larson, P. Mittal, R. Stonecipher, N. Verma, and M. Zwilling. Hekaton: SQL server's memory-optimized OLTP engine. In *SIGMOD*, pages 1243–1254, 2013. DOI: 10.1145/2463676.2463710.

[37] D. Dice, Y. Lev, M. Moir, and D. Nussbaum. Early Experience with a Commercial Hardware Transactional Memory Implementation. In *ASPLOS*, pages 157–168, 2009. DOI: 10.1145/1508244.1508263

[38] J. M. Faleiro and D. J. Abadi. Rethinking serializable multiversion concurrency control. *PVLDB*, 8(11):1190–1201, 2015. DOI: 10.14778/2809974.2809981.

[39] B. Falsafi and D. A. Wood. Reactive NUMA: A design for unifying s-COMA and CC-NUMA. In *ISCA*, pages 229–240, 1997. DOI: 10.1145/384286.264205.

[40] F. Färber, N. May, W. Lehner, P. Gro?e, I. Muller, H. Rauhe, and J. Dees. The SAP HANA database—an architecture overview. *IEEE DEBull*, 35(1):28–33, 2012.

[41] A. Fekete, D. Liarokapis, E. O'Neil, P. O'Neil, and D. Shasha. Making snapshot isolation serializable. *ACM Transactions on Database Systems (TODS)*, 30(2):492–528, 2005. DOI: 10.1145/1071610.1071615.

[42] M. Ferdman, A. Adileh, O. Kocberber, S. Volos, M. Alisafaee, D. Jevdjic, C. Kaynak, A. D. Popescu, A. Ailamaki, and B. Falsafi. Clearing the clouds: A study of emerging scale-out workloads on modern hardware. In *ASPLOS*, pages 37–48, 2012. DOI: 10.1145/2150976.2150982.

[43] M. Ferdman, C. Kaynak, and B. Falsafi. Proactive instruction fetch. In *MICRO*, pages 152–162, 2011. DOI: 10.1145/2155620.2155638.

[44] M. Ferdman, T. F. Wenisch, A. Ailamaki, B. Falsafi, and A. Moshovos. Temporal instruction fetch streaming. In *MICRO*, pages 1–10, 2008. DOI: 10.1109/micro.2008.4771774.

[45] S. Finkelstein. Common Expression Analysis in Database Applications. In *SIGMOD*, pages 235–245, 1982. DOI: 10.1145/582353.582400.

[46] C. Freedman, E. Ismert, and P. Larson. Compilation in the Microsoft SQL Server Hekaton Engine. *IEEE DEBull*, 37(1):22–30, 2014.

[47] K. Gao, S. Harizopoulos, I. Pandis, V. Shkapenyuk, and A. Ailamaki. Simultaneous pipelining in qpipe: Exploiting work sharing opportunities across queries. In *ICDE*, 2006. DOI: 10.1109/icde.2006.138.

[48] G. Giannikis, G. Alonso, and D. Kossmann. SharedDB: Killing one thousand queries with one stone. *PVLDB*, 5(6):526–537, 2012. DOI: 10.14778/2168651.2168654.

[49] G. Giannikis, D. Makreshanski, G. Alonso, and D. Kossmann. Shared workload optimization. *PVLDB*, 7(6):429–440, 2014. DOI: 10.14778/2732279.2732280.

[50] J. Giceva, G. Alonso, T. Roscoe, and T. Harris. Deployment of query plans on multicores. *PVLDB*, 8(3):233–244, November 2014. DOI: 10.14778/2735508.2735513.

[51] G. Graefe, M. Lillibridge, H. Kuno, J. Tucek, and A. Veitch. Controlled lock violation. In *SIGMOD*, pages 85–96, 2013. DOI: 10.1145/2463676.2465325.

[52] N. Hardavellas. The rise and fall of dark silicon. *USENIX*, 2012.

[53] N. Hardavellas, M. Ferdman, B. Falsafi, and A. Ailamaki. Toward dark silicon in servers. *IEEE Micro*, 31(4):6–15, 2011. DOI: 10.1109/mm.2011.77.

[54] N. Hardavellas, I. Pandis, R. Johnson, N. Mancheril, A. Ailamaki, and B. Falsafi. Database servers on chip multiprocessors: Limitations and opportunities. In *CIDR*, pages 79–87, 2007.

[55] S. Harizopoulos and A. Ailamaki. STEPS towards cache-resident transaction processing. In *VLDB*, pages 660–671, 2004. DOI: 10.1016/b978-012088469-8.50059-0.

[56] S. Harizopoulos, V. Shkapenyuk, and A. Ailamaki. QPipe: A simultaneously pipelined relational query engine. In *SIGMOD*, pages 383–394, 2005. DOI: 10.1145/1066157.1066201.

[57] T. Harris and S. Kaestle. Callisto-rts: Fine-grain parallel loops. In *USENIX ATC*, pages 45–56, 2015.

[58] J. M. Hellerstein, M. Stonebraker, and J. Hamilton. Architecture of a database system. *Foundations and Trends (R) in Databases*, 1(2), 2007. DOI: 10.1561/1900000002.

[59] J. L. Hennessy and D. A. Patterson. *Computer Architecture: A Quantitative Approach*. Morgan Kaufmann Publishers Inc., San Francisco, CA, 2002.

[60] M. Herlihy and J. Moss. Transactional Memory: Architectural Support for Lock-free Data Structures. In *ISCA*, pages 289–300, 1993. 10.1145/173682.165164

[61] J. Huang, K. Schwan, and M. K. Qureshi. Nvram-aware logging in transaction systems. *PVLDB*, 8(4):389–400, 2014. DOI: 10.14778/2735496.2735502.

[62] J. Hurwitz, A. Nugent, F. Halper, and M. Kaufman. *Big Data For Dummies*, 1st ed. For Dummies, 2013.

[63] IBM, P. Zikopoulos, and C. Eaton. *Understanding Big Data: Analytics for Enterprise Class Hadoop and Streaming Data*, 1st ed. McGraw-Hill Osborne Media, 2011.

[64] R. Johnson, N. Hardavellas, I. Pandis, N. Mancheril, S. Harizopoulos, K. Sabirli, A. Ailamaki, and B. Falsafi. To share or not to share? In *VLDB*, pages 351–362, 2007.

[65] R. Johnson and I. Pandis. The bionic DBMS is coming, but what will it look like? In *CIDR*, 2013.

[66] R. Johnson, I. Pandis, and A. Ailamaki. Improving OLTP scalability using speculative lock inheritance. *PVLDB*, 2(1):479–489, 2009. DOI: 10.14778/1687627.1687682.

[67] R. Johnson, I. Pandis, and A. Ailamaki. Eliminating unscalable communication in transaction processing. *VLDBJ*, 23(1):1–23, 2014. DOI: 10.1007/s00778-013-0312-3.

[68] R. Johnson, I. Pandis, N. Hardavellas, A. Ailamaki, and B. Falsafi. Shore-MT: A scalable storage manager for the multicore era. In *EDBT*, pages 24–35, 2009. DOI: 10.1145/1516360.1516365.

[69] R. Johnson, I. Pandis, R. Stoica, M. Athanassoulis, and A. Ailamaki. Aether: A scalable approach to logging. *PVLDB*, 3:681–692, 2010. DOI: 10.14778/1920841.1920928.

[70] E. Jones, D. J. Abadi, and S. Madden. Low overhead concurrency control for partitioned main memory databases. In *SIGMOD*, pages 603–614, 2010. DOI: 10.1145/1807167.1807233.

[71] H. Jung, H. Han, A. D. Fekete, G. Heiser, and H. Y. Yeom. A scalable lock manager for multicores. In *SIGMOD*, pages 73–84, 2013. DOI: 10.1145/2463676.2465271.

[72] T. Karnagel, R. Dementiev, R. Rajwar, K. Lai, T. Legler, B. Schlegel, and W. Lehner. Improving in-memory database index performance with intel transactional synchronization extensions. In *HPCA*, pages 476–487, 2014. DOI: 10.1109/hpca.2014.6835957.

[73] M. Karpathiotakis, M. Branco, I. Alagiannis, and A. Ailamaki. Adaptive query processing on raw data. *PVLDB*, 7(12):1119–1130, 2014. DOI: 10.14778/2732977.2732986.

[74] C. Kaynak, B. Grot, and B. Falsafi. SHIFT: Shared history instruction fetch for lean-core server processors. In *MICRO*, pages 272–283, 2013. DOI: 10.1145/2540708.2540732.

[75] K. Keeton, D. A. Patterson, Y. Q. He, R. C. Raphael, and W. E. Baker. Performance characterization of a quad pentium pro SMP using OLTP workloads. In *ISCA*, pages 15–26, 1998. DOI: 10.1109/isca.1998.694759.

[76] A. Kemper and T. Neumann. HyPer: A hybrid OLTP and OLAP main memory database system based on virtual memory snapshots. In *ICDE*, pages 195–206, 2011. DOI: 10.1109/icde.2011.5767867.

[77] T. Kiefer, B. Schlegel, and W. Lehner. Experimental evaluation of NUMA effects on database management systems. In *BTW*, pages 185-204, 2013.

[78] C. Kim, T. Kaldewey, V. W. Lee, E. Sedlar, A. D. Nguyen, N. Satish, J. Chhugani, A. Di Blas, and P. Dubey. Sort vs. hash revisited: Fast join implementation on modern multi-core CPUs. *VLDBJ*, 2(2):1378–1389, 2009. DOI: 10.14778/1687553.1687564.

[79] K. Kim, T. Wang, R. Johnson, and I. Pandis. Ermia: Fast memory-optimized database system for heterogeneous workloads. In *SIGMOD*, pages 1675–1687, 2016. DOI: 10.1145/2882903.2882905.

[80] R. Kimball and M. Ross. *The Data Warehouse Toolkit: The Complete Guide to Dimensional Modeling*, 2nd ed. John Wiley & Sons, Inc., 2002.

[81] H. Kimura. FOEDUS: OLTP engine for a thousand cores and NVRAM. In *SIGMOD*, pages 691–706, 2015. DOI: 10.1145/2723372.2746480.

[82] H. Kimura, G. Graefe, and H. Kuno. Efficient locking techniques for databases on modern hardware. *ADMS*, 2012.

[83] T. Kissinger, T. Kiefer, B. Schlegel, D. Habich, D. Molka, and W. Lehner. ERIS: A NUMA-aware in-memory storage engine for analytical workload. In *International Workshop on Accelerating Data Management Systems Using Modern Processor and Storage Architectures (ADMS)*, pages 74–85, 2014.

[84] Y. Klonatos, C. Koch, T. Rompf, and H. Chafi. Building efficient query engines in a high-level language. *PVLDB*, 7(10):853–864, 2014. DOI: 10.14778/2732951.2732959.

[85] O. Kocberber, B. Grot, J. Picorel, B. Falsafi, K. Lim, and P. Ranganathan. Meet the walkers: Accelerating index traversals for in-memory databases. In *MICRO*, pages 468–479, 2013. DOI: 10.1145/2540708.2540748.

[86] K. Krikellas, S. D. Viglas, and M. Cintra. Generating code for holistic query evaluation. In *ICDE*, pages 613–624, 2010. DOI: 10.1109/ICDE.2010.5447892.

[87] C. Lameter. NUMA (Non-Uniform Memory Access): An Overview. *ACM Queue*, 11(7):40, 2013. 2013. DOI: 10.1145/2508834.2513149.

[88] R. P. LaRowe, Jr., M. A. Holliday, and C. S. Ellis. An analysis of dynamic page placement on a NUMA multiprocessor. In *SIGMETRICS*, pages 23–34, 1992. DOI: 10.1145/133057.133082.

[89] P.-A. Larson, S. Blanas, C. Diaconu, C. Freedman, J. M. Patel, and M. Zwilling. High-performance concurrency control mechanisms for main-memory databases. *PVLDB*, 5(4), pages 298–309, 2011. DOI: 10.14778/2095686.2095689.

[90] J. Lee, Y. S. Kwon, F. Färber, M. Muehle, C. Lee, C. Bensberg, J. Y. Lee, A. H. Lee, and W. Lehner. Sap HANA distributed in-memory database system: Transaction, session, and metadata management. In *ICDE*, pages 1165–1173, 2013. DOI: 10.1109/icde.2013.6544906.

[91] V. Leis, P. Boncz, A. Kemper, and T. Neumann. Morsel-driven parallelism: A NUMA-aware query evaluation framework for the many-core age. In *SIGMOD*, pages 743–754, 2014. DOI: 10.1145/2588555.2610507.

[92] V. Leis, A. Kemper, and T. Neumann. Exploiting hardware transactional memory in main-memory databases. In *ICDE*, pages 580–591, 2014. DOI: 10.1109/icde.2014.6816683.

[93] J. J. Levandoski, D. B. Lomet, and S. Sengupta. The Bw-tree: A b-tree for new hardware platforms. In *ICDE*, pages 302–313, 2013. DOI: 10.1109/icde.2013.6544834.

[94] Y. Li, I. Pandis, R. Mueller, V. Raman, and G. Lohman. NUMA-aware algorithms: The case of data shuffling. In *CIDR*, 2013.

[95] D. Makreshanski, G. Giannikis, G. Alonso, and D. Kossmann. Mqjoin: Efficient shared execution of main-memory joins. *PVLDB*, 9(6):480–491, January 2016. DOI: 10.14778/2904121.2904124.

[96] D. Makreshanski, J. Giceva, C. Barthels, and G. Alonso. BatchDB: Efficient Isolated Execution of Hybrid OLTP+OLAP Workloads for Interactive Applications. In *SIGMOD*, pages 37–50, 2017. DOI: 10.1145/3035918.3035959.

[97] N. Malviya, A. Weisberg, S. Madden, and M. Stonebraker. Rethinking main memory OLTP recovery. In *ICDE*, pages 604–615, 2014. DOI: 10.1109/icde.2014.6816685.

[98] Y. Mao, E. Kohler, and R. T. Morris. Cache craftiness for fast multicore key-value storage. In *EuroSys*, pages 183–196, 2012. DOI: 10.1145/2168836.2168855.

[99] G. Moore. Cramming more components onto integrated circuits. *Electronics*, 38(6), 1965. DOI: 10.1109/jproc.1998.658762.

[100] R. Mueller, J. Teubner, and G. Alonso. Data processing on FPGAs. *PVLDB*, 2(1):910–921, 2009. DOI: 10.14778/1687627.1687730.

[101] H. Mühe, A. Kemper, and T. Neumann. Executing long-running transactions in synchronization-free main memory database systems. In *CIDR*, 2013.

[102] T. Neumann and V. Leis. Compiling database queries into machine code. *IEEE DEBull*, 37(1):3–11, 2014.

[103] T. Neumann, T. Mühlbauer, and A. Kemper. Fast serializable multi-version concurrency control for main-memory database systems. In *SIGMOD*, pages 677–689, 2015. DOI: 10.1145/2723372.2749436.

[104] T. M. Nguyen, J. Schiefer, and A. M. Tjoa. Sense and response service architecture (SARESA): An approach towards a real-time business intelligence solution and its use for a fraud detection application. In *DOLAP*, pages 77–86, 2005. DOI: 10.1145/1097002.1097015.

[105] S. L. Olivier, A. K. Porterfield, K. B. Wheeler, M. Spiegel, and J. F. Prins. OpenMP task scheduling strategies for multicore NUMA systems. *IJHPCA*, 26(2):110–124, May 2012. DOI: 10.1177/1094342011434065.

[106] C. Olofson and H. Morris. Blending transactions and analytics in a single in-memory platform: Key to the real-time enterprise. Technical report, International Data Corporation (IDC), February 2013. IDC 239327.

[107] K. Olukotun, B. A. Nayfeh, L. Hammond, K. Wilson, and K. Chang. The case for a single-chip multiprocessor. In *ASPLOS*, pages 2–11, 1996. DOI: 10.1145/237090.237140.

[108] , I. Pandis, R. Johnson, N. Hardavellas, and A. Ailamaki. Data-Oriented Transaction Execution, *PVLDB*, 3(1):928–939, 2010. DOI: 10.14778/1920841.1920959.

[109] I. Pandis, P. Tözün, R. Johnson, and A. Ailamaki. PLP: Page latch-free shared-everything OLTP. *PVLDB*, 4(10):610–621, 2011. DOI: 10.14778/2021017.2021019.

[110] S. Pelley, T. F. Wenisch, B. T. Gold, and B. Bridge. Storage management in the nvram era. *PVLDB*, 7(2):121-132, 2013. DOI: 10.14778/2732228.2732231.

[111] H. Pirk, E. Petraki, S. Idreos, S. Manegold, and M. Kersten. Database cracking: Fancy scan, not poor man's sort! *DaMoN*, pages 4:1–4:8, 2014. DOI: 10.1145/2619228.2619232.

[112] H. Plattner. A common database approach for OLTP and OLAP using an in-memory column database. In *SIGMOD*, pages 1–2, 2009. DOI: 10.1145/1559845.1559846.

[113] O. Polychroniou, A. Raghavan, and K. A. Ross. Rethinking SIMD vectorization for in-memory databases. In *SIGMOD*, pages 1493–1508, 2015. DOI: 10.1145/2723372.2747645.

[114] O. Polychroniou and K. A. Ross. A comprehensive study of main-memory partitioning and its application to large-scale comparison- and radix-sort. In *SIGMOD*, pages 755–766, 2014. DOI: 10.1145/2588555.2610522.

[115] D. Porobic, E. Liarou, P. Tözün, and A. Ailamaki. ATraPos: Adaptive transaction processing on hardware islands. In *ICDE*, pages 688–699, 2014. DOI: 10.1109/icde.2014.6816692.

[116] D. Porobic, I. Pandis, M. Branco, P. Tözün, and A. Ailamaki. OLTP on hardware islands. *PVLDB*, 5(11):1447–1458, 2012. DOI: 10.14778/2350229.2350260.

[117] D. Porobic, P. Tözün, R. Appuswamy, and A. Ailamaki. More than a network: Distributed OLTP on clusters of hardware islands. In *DaMon*, page 6, 2016. DOI: 10.1145/2933349.2933355.

[118] I. Psaroudakis. *Scaling up concurrent analytical workloads on multi-core servers.* Ph.D. thesis, EPFL IC, 2016.

[119] I. Psaroudakis, M. Athanassoulis, and A. Ailamaki. Sharing data and work across concurrent analytical queries. *PVLDB*, 6(9):637–648, 2013. DOI: 10.14778/2536360.2536364.

[120] I. Psaroudakis, M. Athanassoulis, M. Olma, and A. Ailamaki. Reactive and proactive sharing across concurrent analytical queries. In *SIGMOD*, pages 889–892, 2014. DOI: 10.1145/2588555.2594514.

[121] I. Psaroudakis, T. Kissinger, D. Porobic, T. Ilsche, E. Liarou, P. Tözün, A. Ailamaki, and W. Lehner. Dynamic fine-grained scheduling for energy-efficient main-memory queries. In *DaMoN*, pages 1–7, 2014. DOI: 10.1145/2619228.2619229.

[122] I. Psaroudakis, T. Scheuer, N. May, and A. Ailamaki. Task scheduling for highly concurrent analytical and transactional main-memory workloads. In *ADMS*, pages 36–45, 2013.

[123] I. Psaroudakis, T. Scheuer, N. May, A. Sellami, and A. Ailamaki. Scaling up concurrent main-memory column-store scans: Towards adaptive NUMA-aware data and task placement. *PVLDB*, 8(12):1442–1453, 2015. DOI: 10.14778/2824032.2824043.

[124] I. Psaroudakis, T. Scheuer, N. May, A. Sellami, and A. Ailamaki. Adaptive NUMA-aware data placement and task scheduling for analytical workloads in main-memory column-stores. *PVLDB*, 10(2):37–48, 2016. DOI: 10.14778/3015274.3015275.

[125] I. Psaroudakis, F. Wolf, N. May, T. Neumann, A. Böhm, A. Ailamaki, and K.-U. Sattler. Scaling up mixed workloads: A battle of data freshness, flexibility, and scheduling. In *TPCTC*, pages 97–112. DOI: 10.1007/978-3-319-15350-6.

[126] A. Putnam, A. M. Caulfield, E. S. Chung, D. Chiou, K. Constantinides, J. Demme, H. Esmaeilzadeh, J. Fowers, G. P. Gopal, J. Gray, M. Haselman, S. Hauck, S. Heil, A. Hormati, J.-Y. Kim, S. Lanka, J. Larus, E. Peterson, S. Pope, A. Smith, J. Thong,

P. Y. Xiao, and D. Burger. A reconfigurable fabric for accelerating large-scale datacenter services. In *ISCA*, pages 13–24, 2014. DOI: 10.1109/isca.2014.6853195.

[127] L. Qiao, V. Raman, F. Reiss, P. J. Haas, and G. M. Lohman. Main-memory scan sharing for multi-core CPUs. *PVLDB*, 1(1):610-621, 2008. DOI: 10.14778/1453856.1453924.

[128] R. Rajwar and J. Goodman. Speculative Lock Elision: Enabling Highly Concurrent Multithreaded Execution. *MICRO*, pages 294–305, 2001.

[129] R. Ramakrishnan and J. Gehrke. *Database Management Systems*. McGraw-Hill, Inc., New York, NY, 2003.

[130] V. Raman, G. Swart, L. Qiao, F. Reiss, V. Dialani, D. Kossmann, I. Narang, and R. Sidle. Constant-time query processing. In *ICDE*, pages 60–69, 2008. DOI: 10.1109/icde.2008.4497414.

[131] A. Ramirez, L. A. Barroso, K. Gharachorloo, R. Cohn, J. Larriba-Pey, P. G. Lowney, and M. Valero. Code layout optimizations for transaction processing workloads. In *ISCA*, pages 155–164, 2001. DOI: 10.1145/379240.379260.

[132] P. Ranganathan, K. Gharachorloo, S. V. Adve, and L. A. Barroso. Performance of database workloads on shared-memory systems with out-of-order processors. In *ASPLOS*, pages 307–318, 1998. DOI: 10.1145/384265.291067.

[133] K. Ren, A. Thomson, and D. J. Abadi. An evaluation of the advantages and disadvantages of deterministic database systems. *PVLDB*, 7(10):821-832, 2014. DOI: 10.14778/2732951.2732955.

[134] K. A. Ross. Selection conditions in main memory. *ACM TODS*, 29(1):132–161, 2004. DOI: 10.1145/974750.974755.

[135] N. Roussopoulos. View indexing in relational databases. *ACM TODS*, 7(2):258–290, 1982. DOI: 10.1145/319702.319729.

[136] G. M. Sacco and M. Schkolnick. Buffer management in relational database systems. *ACM TODS*, 11(4):473–498, 1986. DOI: 10.1145/7239.7336.

[137] N. Satish, C. Kim, J. Chhugani, A. D. Nguyen, V. W. Lee, D. Kim, and P. Dubey. Fast sort on CPUs and GPUs: A case for bandwidth oblivious SIMD sort. In *SIGMOD*, pages 351–362, 2010. DOI: 10.1145/1807167.1807207.

[138] T. K. Sellis. Multiple-query optimization. *ACM TODS*, 13(1):23–52, 1988. DOI: 10.1145/42201.42203.

[139] J. Sewall, J. Chhugani, C. Kim, N. Satish, and P. Dubey. PALM: Parallel architecture-friendly latch-free modifications to b+trees on many-core processors. *PVLDB*, 4(11):795–806, 2011.

[140] J. Shim, P. Scheuermann, and R. Vingralek. Dynamic caching of query results for decision support systems. In *SSDBM*, 1999. DOI: 10.1109/ssdm.1999.787641.

[141] U. Sirin, P. Tözün, D. Porobic, and A. Ailamaki. Micro-architectural analysis of in-memory OLTP. In *SIGMOD*, pages 387–402, 2016. DOI: 10.1145/2882903.2882916.

[142] E. Sitaridi, O. Polychroniou, and K. A. Ross. Simd-accelerated regular expression matching. In *DaMoN*, 2016. DOI: 10.1145/2933349.2933357.

[143] S. Somogyi, T. F. Wenisch, A. Ailamaki, and B. Falsafi. Spatio-temporal memory streaming. In *ISCA*, pages 69–80, 2009. DOI: 10.1145/1555754.1555766.

[144] P. Stenström, T. Joe, and A. Gupta. Comparative performance evaluation of cache-coherent NUMA and COMA architectures. In *ISCA*, pages 80–91, 1992. DOI: 10.1109/isca.1992.753306.

[145] R. Stets, K. Gharachorloo, and L. A. Barroso. A detailed comparison of two transaction processing workloads. In *WWC*, pages 37–48, 2002. DOI: 10.1109/wwc.2002.1226492.

[146] M. Stonebraker, S. Madden, D. J. Abadi, S. Harizopoulos, N. Hachem, and P. Helland. The end of an architectural era: (It's time for a complete rewrite). In *VLDB*, pages 1150–1160, 2007.

[147] M. Stonebraker and A. Weisberg. The VoltDB main memory DBMS. *IEEE DEBull*, 36(2):21–27, 2013.

[148] A. Thomson and D. J. Abadi. The case for determinism in database systems. *PVLDB*, 3(1-2):70-80 , 2010. DOI: 10.14778/1920841.1920855.

[149] A. Thomson, T. Diamond, S.-C. Weng, K. Ren, P. Shao, and D. J. Abadi. Calvin: Fast distributed transactions for partitioned database systems. In *SIGMOD*, pages 1–12, 2012. DOI: 10.1145/2213836.2213838.

[150] P. Tözün, I. Atta, A. Ailamaki, and A. Moshovos. ADDICT: Advanced instruction chasing for transactions. *PVLDB*, 7(14):1893–1904, 2014. DOI: 10.14778/2733085.2733095.

[151] P. Tözün, B. Gold, and A. Ailamaki. OLTP in wonderland—Where do cache misses come from in major OLTP components? In *DaMoN*, pages 8:1–8:6, 2013. DOI: 10.1145/2485278.2485286.

[152] P. Tözün, I. Pandis, C. Kaynak, D. Jevdjic, and A. Ailamaki. From A to E: Analyzing TPC's OLTP benchmarks—the obsolete, the ubiquitous, the unexplored. In *EDBT*, pages 17–28, 2013. DOI: 10.1145/2452376.2452380.

[153] TPC Benchmark B Standard Specification, 1994. http://www.tpc.org/tpcb

[154] TPC Benchmark C Standard Specification, 2010. http://www.tpc.org/tpcc

[155] TPC Benchmark D Standard Specification, 1998. http://www.tpc.org/tpcd

[156] TPC Benchmark E Standard Specification, 2014. http://www.tpc.org/tpce

[157] K. Q. Tran, S. Blanas, and J. F. Naughton. On transactional memory, spinlocks, and database transactions. In *ADMS*, pages 43–50, 2010.

[158] S. Tu, W. Zheng, E. Kohler, B. Liskov, and S. Madden. Speedy transactions in multicore in-memory databases. In *SOSP*, pages 18–32, 2013. DOI: 10.1145/2517349.2522713.

[159] B. Vikranth, R. Wankar, and C. R. Rao. Topology aware task stealing for on-Chip NUMA multi-core processors. In *ICCS*, pages 379–388, 2013. DOI: 10.1016/j.procs.2013.05.201.

[160] S. Wanderman-Milne and N. Li. Runtime Code Generation in Cloudera Impala. *IEEE DEBull*, 37(1):31–37, 2014.

[161] A. Wang, M. Gaudet, P. Wu, J. Amaral, M. Ohmacht, C. Barton, R. Silvera, and M. Michael. Evaluation of Blue Gene/Q Hardware Support for Transactional Memories. In *PACT*, pages 127–136, 2012.

[162] T. Wang and R. Johnson. Scalable logging through emerging non-volatile memory. *PVLDB*, 7(10):865–876, 2014. DOI: 10.14778/2732951.2732960.

[163] Z. Wang, H. Qian, J. Li, and H. Chen. Using restricted transactional memory to build a scalable in-memory database. In *Eurosys*, pages 26:1–26:15, 2014. DOI: 10.1145/2592798.2592815.

[164] K. M. Wilson and B. B. Aglietti. Dynamic page placement to improve locality in CC-NUMA multiprocessors for TPC-C. In *SC*, pages 33–33, 2001. DOI: 10.1145/582034.582067.

[165] S. Wolf, H. Mühe, A. Kemper, and T. Neumann. An evaluation of strict timestamp ordering concurrency control for main-memory database systems. In *IMDM*, pages 82–93. 2013. DOI: 10.1007/978-3-319-13960-9_7.

[166] L. Wu, A. Lottarini, T. K. Paine, M. A. Kim, and K. A. Ross. Q100: The architecture and design of a database processing unit. In *ASPLOS*, pages 255–268, 2014. DOI: 10.1145/2541940.2541961.

[167] J. Wust, M. Grund, K. Hoewelmeyer, D. Schwalb, and H. Plattner. *Concurrent Execution of Mixed Enterprise Workloads on In-memory Databases*, pages 126–140. Springer International Publishing, 2014. DOI: 10.1007/978-3-319-05810-8_9.

[168] X. Yu, G. Bezerra, A. Pavlo, S. Devadas, and M. Stonebraker. Staring into the abyss: An evaluation of concurrency control with one thousand cores. *PVLDB*, 8(3):209–220, 2014. DOI: 10.14778/2735508.2735511.

[169] X. Yu, A. Pavlo, D. Sanchez, and S. Devadas. Tictoc: Time traveling optimistic concurrency control. In *SIGMOD*, pages 1629–1642, 2016. DOI: 10.1145/2882903.2882935.

[170] Y. Yuan, K. Wang, R. Lee, X. Ding, J. Xing, S. Blanas, and X. Zhang. BCC: Reducing false aborts in optimistic concurrency control with low cost for in-memory databases. *PVLDB*, 9(6):504–515, 2016. DOI: 10.14778/2904121.2904126.

[171] J. Zhou, J. Cieslewicz, K. A. Ross, and M. Shah. Improving database performance on simultaneous multithreading processors. In *VLDB*, pages 49–60, 2005.

[172] J. Zhou and K. A. Ross. Implementing database operations using SIMD instructions. In *SIGMOD*, pages 145–156, 2002. DOI: 10.1145/564691.564709.

[173] R. Francis and I. Mathieson. A Benchmark Parallel Sort for Shared Memory Multiprocessors. *IEEE Trans. Computers*, 37(12):1619–1626, 1988. DOI: 10.1109/12.9738.

[174] S. Idreos, M. L. Kersten and S. Manegold Database Cracking. *CIDR*, pages 68–78, 2007.

Authors' Biographies

ANASTASIA AILAMAKI

Anastasia Ailamaki is a Professor of Computer and Communication Sciences at the École Polytechnique Fédérale de Lausanne (EPFL) in Switzerland. Her research interests are in data-intensive systems and applications, and in particular (a) in strengthening the interaction between the database software and emerging hardware and I/O devices, and (b) in automating data anagement to support computationally-demanding, data-intensive scientific applications. She has received an ERC Consolidator Award (2013), a Finmeccanica endowed chair from the Computer Science Department at Carnegie Mellon (2007), a European Young Investigator Award from the European Science Foundation (2007), an Alfred P. Sloan Research Fellowship (2005), eight best-paper awards in database, storage, and computer architecture conferences (2001-2012), and an NSF CAREER award (2002). She holds a Ph.D. in Computer Science from the University of Wisconsin-Madison in 2000. She is an ACM fellow and the vice chair of the ACM SIGMOD community, as well as a senior member of the IEEE. She has served as a CRA-W mentor and is a member of the Expert Network of the World Economic Forum.

ERIETTA LIAROU

Erietta Liarou

Erietta Liarou is currently a co-founder in a data analytics startup. She received her Ph.D. in Computer Science from University of Amsterdam in 2013. In her thesis she worked on the first column-store stream processing system, MonetDB/DataCell, that leverages analytical systems technology for scalable stream processing. Her research interests include database architectures, transaction processing on modern hardware, data-stream processing and distributed query processing. In the past she has been with the Data-Intensive Applications and Systems Laboratory (DIAS) in EPFL, the Dutch National Research Center for Mathematics and Computer Science (CWI) in Amsterdam, The Netherlands, the Intelligence Systems Laboratory in Technical University of Crete, Greece, and with the System S group in IBM T.J.Watson Research Center, Hawthorne, NY, USA. In 2011, she received the Best Paper Award in Challenges and Visions at the Very Large Database Conference.

PINAR TÖZÜN

Pınar Tözün is a research staff member at IBM Almaden Research Center. Before joining IBM, she received her Ph.D. from EPFL. Her research focuses on HTAP engines, performance characterization of database workloads, and scalability and efficiency of data management systems on modern hardware. She received a Jim Gray Doctoral Dissertation Award Honorable Mention in 2016. During her Ph.D., she also spent a summer in Oracle Labs (Redwood Shores, CA) as an intern. Before starting her Ph.D., she received her BSc degree in Computer Engineering department of Koç University in 2009.

DANICA POROBIC

Danica Porobic is a Principal Member of Technical Staff at Oracle working on the database in-memory technologies. She received her Ph.D. from EPFL where she focused on designing scalable transaction processing systems for non-uniform hardware. She has graduated top of her class with MSc and BSc in Informatics from University of Novi Sad and has worked at Oracle Labs and Microsoft SQL Server.

IRAKLIS PSAROUDAKIS

Iraklis Psaroudakis is a Senior Member of Technical Staff at Oracle Labs. His research interests include improving the performance of analytical workloads, parallel programming, and OS/runtime-system interaction. Prior to Oracle, he completed his Ph.D. at the Data-Intensive Application and Systems (DIAS) Laboratory of the École Polytechnique Fédérale de Lausanne (EPFL), focusing on scaling up highly concurrent analytical database workloads on multi-socket multi-core servers through (a) sharing data and work across concurrent queries, and (b) adaptive NUMA-aware data placement and task scheduling. During his Ph.D., he cooperated with the SAP HANA database team. Before starting his Ph.D., he completed his studies in Electrical & Computer Engineering at the National Technical University of Athens (NTUA).

Printed in the United States
by Baker & Taylor Publisher Services